The Unknown World of the Ming Court Painters:

The Ming Painting Academy

日近清光

The Unknown the Ming Court Painters:

The Ming Painting Academy

日近清光

By Hou-mei Sung

宋后楣 著

The Liberal Arts Press
文史哲出版社印行

*first edition *500 copies*

Additional copies auailable through
The Liberal Arts Press
4,LANE 72,ROOSEVELT ROAD, SEC. 1
TAIPEI, TAIWAN, REPUBLIC OF CHINA

The Unknown World of the Ming Court Painters:

The Ming Painting Academy

Table of Contents

Foreword

The manuscript of this book was first completed in 1998 as part of a larger research and teaching project, which comprised of two parts. The first part focuses on the reconstruction of many leading Ming court painters' biographies as well as the political and ethical issues that concerned the Ming court. The second part intends to use animal paintings created in the Ming court to illustrate how the change in the painters' status further served to reshape the functions of their paintings. I have since decided to publish the first part concerning the institutional history of the Ming Painting Academy separately, as most of the contents of the second part will be featured in a special exhibition on Chinese animal painting and published in the exhibition catalogue.

I would like to thank the Center for Chinese Studies, Taiwan, Republic of China, and the Fulbright Exchange scholar Fellowship Program for their generous contributions in the funding of the research for this book. I am also deeply grateful to Dr. Mette Siggstedt and Ms. Koto Ishida for reading the manuscript and giving me helpful suggestions.

Introduction

The Ming court painters, who played an important role in setting new trends in painting, until recently, had been so poorly represented in Chinese art history that today there is hardly any information on either their lives or works. Even less is known about the Ming Painting Academy. When and how was the Ming Painting Academy formed? How was the Ming Painting Academy structured? What recruitment and promotion procedures did the Ming court painters utilize? Which types of official titles were used? And, finally, what led to the collapse of the organization in the late Ming? The lack of information on so many aspects of the institution has led many scholars to question its very existence.[1]

New revelations about the organization the Ming court painters and their achievements have important implications for our understanding of Ming painting history, and indeed, the entire history of Chinese painting. More than a dynastic link in Chinese painting history, the early Ming court painters' revival and reinterpretation of the Tang and Song court traditions - following the Mongolian ruled Yuan dynasty - formed a bridge to a badly disrupted past. Ironically, it was through the effort to reconnect with the past that a

---

[1] For past research on the Ming Painting Academy and court painters, see Harry Vanderstappen, "Painters at the Early Ming Court and the Problem of a Ming Painting Academy," *Monumenta Serica*, v. 15 (1956), pp. 259-302 and v. 16 (1957), pp. 315-347; Suzuki Kei, "Concerning the Organization of the Ming Painting Academy," *Bijutsushi*, v. 15, no. 4 (March 1955), pp. 95-106; and Hou-mei Sung, "The Formation of the Ming Painting Academy," *Ming Studies*, no. 29 (Spring, 1991)(quoted as "Ming Painting Academy"); James Cahill, *Parting at the Shore:Chinese Painting of the Early and Middle Ming Dynasty, 1368-1580*, pp. 3-56; Richard Barnhart, *Painters of the Great Ming: The Imperial Court and the Zhe School*, pp. 1-19.

completely new institution emerged.

This book addresses the numerous unresolved questions surrounding the early and mid Ming court painters and their Painting Academy. Included in the discussion here are new findings on the formation and major structural changes of the Painting Academy in the late Yongle (1403-1424) and early Xuande (1426-1435) eras, the infiltration of military artisans in the Painting Academy after the Zhengtong era (1436-1449), and the special patronage and irregular promotion of court painters in the Chenghua era (1465-1487).

It is necessary to point out here that the fundamental changes of the Ming Painting Academy were closely linked to a broad range of political, social, and institutional changes of the Ming court. It is beyond the scope of this preliminary study to cover the full extent of its development. Also excluded is the discussion of the changed function of the Ming court painting -- manifested in their new approaches in styles, iconographies, technical qualities, inscriptions by literati, and the painters' creation of a politically motivated symbolic language using numerous old and new themes – as this has been covered in a separate project.[2]

The Chinese title of the book, *Rijin qingguang* (Daily Approaching the Pure Radiance) was taken from the reading of an imperial seal awarded to leading masters serving in the Painting Academy during the Chenghua and Hongzhi eras. It aptly sums up the Ming court painters' new status in court once the Painting Academy became an attachment of Yuyongjian (Directorate of Imperial Accouterments) and all its members personal employees of the emperor.

---

[2] See Hou-mei Sung, "The Symbolic Language of Chinese Animal Painting" (the finished manuscript is pending for publication).

Chapter One

The Formation of the Ming Painting Academy

Much of the confusion and controversy concerning the existence of the Ming Painting Academy was caused by the fact that the Ming organization had undergone such revolutionary changes from its Song predecessor that it is hardly recognizable without a new definition. Unlike its Song predecessors, the Ming Painting Academy was no longer an independent institution affiliated with the prestigious Hanlin Academy, but an attachment of the eunuch controlled Yuyongjian (Directorate for Imperial Accouterments). This fundamental change was the defining moment in the Ming Painting Academy and it engendered new distinctive structures and functions, which will be the focus of the discussion here.

Although the Ming Painting Academy was not formed until the late Yongle era, the Ming court painters were destined for a new status when the Hongwu emperor abolished the central administrative agency of Zhongshusheng (Secretariat) in 1380. Zhongshusheng had been the core of administration of the early Ming government, supervising numerous affairs, including those of the court painters. This is evidenced by the following account concerning Zhao Yuan in *Wusheng shishi*:

"During the Hongwu era, painters were gathered in the Zhongshu and ordered to paint the portrait of ancient sages and heroes. Zhao Yuan offended the emperor and was executed."[3]

Also affected by the 1380 restructuring of the Ming government was the status of Zhongshu sheren (Secretariat Drafter), a position held by many early Ming painters. The title underwent many changes in the Ming and caused a great deal of confusion in later research.[4] It is essential here to distinguish how those who were offered the title before 1380 differed from those who received it after that year. The two painters who received the Zhongshu sheren title before 1380 were Zhu Fei and Shen Xiyuan. It is clear that Zhu was not honored with the title for his skills as a painter. During the early Hongwu era, prior to his promotion to Zhongshu sheren in 1376, Zhu was serving as a Hanlin bianxiu (Compiler in the Hanlin Academy). In addition, it was clearly specified when Zhu was promoted that he was qualified by virtue of his knowledge of the classics and his calligraphy skill. Nor did Shen serve in court solely in the capacity of a painter, even though he was rewarded his title after pleasing the emperor with an imperial portrait.[5]

Adding to the confusion of the Zhongshu sheren title was the fact that in the later Yongle era, this title was given to a group of calligraphers serving as drafters. They were mostly talented young scholars recommended by prominent scholar officials and supervised by Huang Huai, the Grand Secretary in Wenyuange (Hall of Literary Profundity). Their major duty was to assist the Grand Secretaries with copying work. Occasionally, they also participated in copying sutras and writing title pieces for imperial halls or palaces. Many of the calligraphers were also scholar painters, including Wang Fu, Xia Chang, and Chen Zongyuan. Their close association with the Hanlin officials elevated their social status and they should be differentiated from not only the court painters, but also the artisan-calligraphers serving in the Wenhua hall in the later Xuande era, which was modeled after the Shuyiju

---

[3] Jiang Shaoshu, *Wusheng shishi, juan* 1, p. 6.
[4] See Hou-mei Sung, "Ming Painting Academy."
[5] See *Minghualu, juan* 1, p. 6.

(Calligrapher Service) of the Song dynasty.

Although there was a great demand for painters at the beginning of the new era for making imperial portraits and decorating new palace buildings, most painters recruited to the Hongwu court were only temporarily employed and never received any official titles. They were identified as huagong (artisan painter) and were not differentiated from other artisans. The one exception is Chen Yuan, who received the title Wenyuange daizhao (Painter-in-attendance in the Wenyuan Pavilion) after he pleased the emperor with an imperial portrait in 1370. Chen's title appears to be an isolated case. This is evidenced by the fact that in that same year Sun Wenzong was summoned for the same purpose but received no title.[6] The special honor was offered to Chen mainly because he was the younger brother of Chen Yu, the most trusted and respected advisor of the emperor.

Thus, it can be concluded that other than a few privileged individuals, most Hongwu painters were summoned for special commissions and received no official titles. They were given the same status as artisans and their activities were limited to painting wall decorations and imperial portraits.

Historians discussing the Ming Painting Academy typically started from the Xuande era and ignored the previous Yongle era (1403-1424). Yet recent research reveals that the initial structure of the Ming Painting Academy originated in the late Yongle era. The Yongle emperor was far more educated and skillful than his father in using art to promote his political needs. In fact, in the very beginning of his reign, the Yongle emperor made an attempt to restore both the Huayuan (Painting Academy) and Shuyuan (Academy of Calligraphy) in the Hanlin Academy. In 1404, he ordered Huang Huai to carry out this task. For the Shuyuan, Huang selected twenty-eight calligraphers from the recruited drafters. They were given masterpieces from the imperial collection as models for their daily exercises and encouraged to practice the

---

[6] For biographies of Chen Yuan and Sun Wenzong, see *Chongguo meishujia renming cidian*, p. 1036.

calligraphic styles of Wang Xizhi and his son, Wang Xianzhi. The collective training eventually led this group to form a distinctive style of calligraphy known as Guangeti (Academician style). Although this calligrapher group in the Yongle court was never formally called Shuyuan and could not match its Song predecessor in scale, it was established with the intention of forming an institution of the same nature. For the Huayuan, Huang recruited Guo Wentong (later Guo Chun) from his hometown Yongjia. However, the founding of the Painting Academy failed to materialize at this point because of the emperor's northern expedition. Guo stayed and served in court without any official title.

Unfortunately, in 1413 Huang suffered a severe blow to his career and was jailed for ten years. Huang's departure had negative effects for Guo's career. However, one evening near the end of the following year the emperor saw a masterpiece by Guo and was so deeply impressed that he immediately summoned the artist the next morning and introduced him to three Ministers from the Ministries of Works (Gongbu), War (Bingbu), and Revenue (Hubu). The emperor then offered Guo the new name, Chun (Sincere), as an indication of his virtue, the official title of Yingshansuo cheng (Director of the Work Project Office, 7a) and many gifts.[7]

This incident, recorded by Huang Huai, is extremely important for our understanding of both Guo's personal career and the initial structure of the Ming Painting Academy. The assignment of Yingshansuo cheng to Guo, who was the first painter recruited for the Ming Painting Academy, signifies also the initial official recognition of the court painters. The fact that the emperor deemed it necessary to confer with all three Ministers shows the complexities of Guo's official status in court. The Minister of Works was involved because Yingshansuo[8] was a subsection in his Ministry. The Minister of Revenue was

---

[7] See Hou-mei Sung, "Ming Painting Academy."

[8] For Yingshansuo, see Charles O. Hucker, *A Dictionary of Official Titles in Imperial China*, p. 583 and Hou-mei Sung, "Ming Painting Academy."

notified because the imperial order specified that Guo's title was not functional and was used only to indicate his salary. In other words, instead of serving in the Ministry of Work as a laborer, Guo was to serve in Yuyongjian (Directorate for Imperial Accouterments) as a painter. Finally, the Minister of War was consulted because Guo was still registered in the Military Guard Unit of Xingwu.[9]

The title Yingshansuo cheng that Guo received was soon extended to all other senior painters in the Yongle court. This is documented by a poem of Lu Yi (1439 -1489) lamenting the death of Fan Xian, a painter who served in the Yongle court for over thirty years. Lu wrote:

"Formerly a Diziyuan (government student), he (Fan Xian) enjoyed painting flowers, which were extremely lovely. Yao Guangxiao, the Shaoshi (Preceptor Junior) was going to recommend him to the Huayuan (Painting Academy). Unfortunately, Fan was an associate of Zhu Yan, who, with all his wealth, returned to the pit and left his wild ambition unaccomplished. During all this time, (Fan's) painting withered and he became the only one not promoted to the Yingshan position." Lu then added a note saying that at one point all of the court painters were awarded with an official title in the Yingshansuo, but Qidong (Fan Xian) was excluded."[10]

The above poem appears intentionally vague concerning Fan's patron, Zhu Yan, whose name is not found in any of the Ming biographies. Lu hinted that Fan's involvement with Zhu, who perished for unspecified reason, was the cause of Fan's failure to join the other court painters when they were all promoted to the Yingshansuo cheng. Despite the unclear relationship between Zhu and Fan, Lu pointed out that Yao Guangxiao (1335-1418) intended to recommended Fan to the Painting Academy. As Yao died in 1418 (the sixteenth year of the Yongle era), the Painting Academy Lu referred to must

---

[9]   See "Gemenshi Guogong muzhiming" by Huang Huai in *Jieanji* (in *Jingxianglou congshu*), *juan* 9, pp. 16-17.
[10]   See Lu Yi, *Chunyü tanggao, juan* 4, pp. 2-3 and Hou-mei Sung, "Ming Painting Academy", pp. 45-46.

have been established before 1417. The same applies to all the senior painters' promotion to Yingshansuo cheng.

The Yongle emperor's decision to promote all senior painters to the title of Yingshansuo cheng and place them under the supervision of Yuyongjian marked the formation of the initial structure of the Ming Painting Academy. Strengthening this theory is the fact that Guo's promotion coincides with the Yongle emperor's second trip to Beijing (from 1413 to1414), which is a major operation in moving the government from Nanjing to Beijing.[11] The numerous officials and court painters who participated in this imperial trip did not return with the emperor in 1414, but stayed in Beijing.[12] Viewed in this historical context, the Yongle emperor's official recognition of Guo and other court painters and their loosely organized structure under Yuyongjian in 1414 signify an opportunistic event to inaugurate both the newly relocated court and the birth of the Ming Painting Academy.

The two other painters known to have served in the Yongle court are Bian Wenjin and Xie Huan. Recent research reveals that Bian was first recruited to Wensiyuan (Craft Institute) as a Fushi (Vice Commissioner). So he was likely among the group of senior painters promoted to Yingshansuo cheng shortly after 1414 of the Yongle era.[13]

Xie Huan was probably recruited by Huang Huai, since both came from Yongjia and Huang was also a patron of Xie's teacher Chen Shugi. Although no information is available on his official status before the Xuande

---

[11] Although Beijing was not officially declared the new capitol until 1420, preparation for the move had begun since the very beginning of the era. See *Ming taizong shilu, juan* 16, p. 2 and *juan* 89, p.3, and Edward L. Farmer, *Early Ming Government: The Evolution of Dual Capitals* (Harvard University Press, 1976).

[12] Evidences for the three artists' participation in the imperial trip to Beijing from 1413 to 1416 are deduced from their biographical information found in various sources. For Guo Chun, see: Huang Huai, *Jieanji, juan* 9, pp. 16-17. For Bian Wenjin, see Houmei Sung, "Bian Wenjin and His Flower-and-bird Painting," Oriental Art, v. XXXVIII, no. 3 (Autumn 1992), pp. 154-164; and for Xie Huan, see Hu Yan, *Yian wenxuan, juan shang*, pp. 81-83.

[13] Bian's career ended in 1427 when he was stripped of his official title as Wuyingdian daizhao. See *Mingshilu, Xuanzong shilu, juan* 23, p. 8. The title Wuyingdian youshunmeng daizhao was first installed in the second month of 1425, see *Mingshilu, Renzong shilu, juan* 7, p. 3.

era, it is most likely that Xie was also among the group of senior painters promoted to Yingshansuo cheng. Judging from the fact that Xie was promoted first to Jinyiwei baihu (Platoon Commander of the Embroidered Uniform Guard, 6a) and then Qianhu (Battalion Commander, 5a) in the Xuande era, he probably reached a senior status by the end of the Yongle era.[14]

Although the Yongle emperor was responsible for the formation of the basic structure of the Ming Painting Academy attached to Yuyongjian, the formal installation of the Painting Academy in a specific location and the full-fledged ranking and operation system both awaited Emperor Xuanzong, an emperor who not only enjoyed painting, but was also an accomplished painter himself. As the discussion below will demonstrate, Xuanzong's instrumental role in shaping the Ming Painting Academy can be traced to his heir-apparent days. His first step toward formalizing the Painting Academy was giving it a designated location. Before the Xuande reign, court painters had no specific place to conduct their work. This is revealed by the fact that when Guo Chun was first recruited to the court, he was not assigned to any office and had to work temporarily in the Wulou (Military Tower). Even in the following reign of Renzong, most painters were assigned to different halls. For instance, in 1425, Guo Chun was assigned to Xihua Gate and Bian Wenjin to Wuying Hall.[15] Thus, it was a significant event when Emperor Xuanzong designated Renzhi Hall as the location of his Painting Academy. This specific location was mentioned by Qiu Jun (1418-95), who wrote: "In front of the Renzhi Hall the Painting Academy was established. It demands thousands of olls of silk from Exi." [16] Probably referring to the same new facility is an account in *Xuanzong shilu* (The Veritable Record of Xuanzong) relating that

---

[14] For discussion on Xie Huan's biography and painting, see Hou-mei Sung, "From the Min-Che Tradition to the Che School, Part 2: Precursors of the Che School, Hsieh Huan and Tai Chin" *the National Palace Museum Research Quarterly*, v. 7, no. 1 (1989), pp. 6-10.(cited as "Min-Che, Part 2."

[15] See Hou-mei Sung, "Ming Painting Academy."

[16] See Qiu Jün (1418-1495), *Qiongtaigao, juan* 6, p. 13.

in 1428, the emperor built a new workshop for Yuyongjian.[17]

Equally important is Xuanzong's promotion of the senior painters in the Painting Academy to the military ranks of Jinyiwei, the prestigious imperial bodyguard unit. The Jinyiwei titles offered to the court painters were nonfunctional but indicated the painters' higher salary and status.

From the above discussion, it is clear that the first generation of Ming court painters - beginning with Guo Chun - started their service shortly after the Yongle era around 1404. After 1414, when the court painters moved to Beijing, they were formally organized under the Yuyongjian. Court painters were often first recruited to the institution of Wensiyuan, supervised by the eunuchs of the Yuyongjian. They typically served for a period of time without any official titles. After this sort of probationary period, those who met the approval of the emperor would receive a minimum monthly ration of rice and guandai (official hat and belt) as the official token of a court painter. The initial titles for them in Wensiyuan were Fushi (Vice Commissioner, 9b) and Dashi (Commissioner-in-chief, 9a). They would then be promoted to Yingshansuo (Work Project Office), another agency supervised by the eunuchs of Yuyongjian, where their title would first be the Suofu (Deputy Director, 7b) and Suocheng (Director, 7a).

Beginning in the Xuande era, painters who graduated from the ranks of Wensiyüan and Yingshansuo were able to enter a higher salary rating system. The ascending ranks include Suozhenfu (Battalion Judge, 6b), Baihu (Platoon Commander, 6a), Fuqianhu (Vice Battalion Commander 5b), Zhengqianhu (Battalion Commander, 5a), Weizhenfu (Guard Judge, 5b), Zhihui qianshi (Assistant Commander, 4a), Zhihui tongzhi (Vice Commander, 3b), and Zhihuishi (Commander, 3a).

---

[17]   See Ming*xüanzong Shilu, juan* 9, p. 16.

Chapter Two

The Mid Ming Painting Academy

The fundamentally changed Ming Painting Academy formed in the early Ming era soon took a new turn in its development and evolved into an even more foreign institution. The root of the new development lies in the social backgrounds of the Ming court painters.

The Rise of Military Artisans in the Ming Court

From the very beginning of the Ming era, the entire population was divided in hereditary classes based on occupation. The two largest classes were <u>min</u> (civilian) and <u>jün</u> (military). Ming artisans also included <u>minjiang</u> (civilian artisans) and <u>jünjiang</u> (military artisans). The establishment of the <u>Jünjiang</u> organization within the military system was a unique feature of the Ming military system. Its origin can be traced to 1389, when the Hongwu emperor first ordered the <u>Wujün dudufu</u> (Five Chief Military Commissions) to send officials to their designated military garrisons and establish bureaus of military artisans. The recruiting method was to choose four candidates out of every one hundred military families. Additional members were chosen from the physically weak and less capable members of the military personnel. All candidates then received one year of training in various skills and crafts before they became formal members of the <u>Jünjiang</u>. The function of the military artisans was to supply all the necessities of the military and thus relieve the civilians of such burden.[18]

As early as the Yongle era, artisan painters from both civilian and military backgrounds were recruited to the Ming court. The very first Ming court painter with a military background is Guo Chun. Guo's family was registered with the military guard unit of Xingwu, yet he was released from the military registration through the imperial order of Xuanzong.[19] Starting from the late Yongle era, an influx of court painters with military artisan background began to dominate the Painting Academy. Unfortunately, this outstanding and extremely important feature of the Ming Painting Academy has never been recognized or studied in the past. In the following discussion, I will focus on the Ming military artisan painters' lineage, their infiltration into the Ming Painting Academy, their ranking system, and how they changed the course of development of Ming court painting.

Before the Yongle era, military artisans were relatively small in number and limited in their specialties. But after the Yongle era, with the emperor's constant northern campaigns, the relocation of the government from Nanjing to Beijing, and the many large-scaled construction projects and repairs needed in Beijing, military artisans were in great demand. The sharp increase in their numbers triggered changes in their organization and function.

The Ming military artisans can be divided into two categories: 1) those serving in the Wugong (Military Merit) units (Wugong zhongwei, Wugong zuowei and Wugong youwei) and 2) those serving in the imperial bodyguard units of Jinyiwei (Embroidered Uniform Guard), Fujun qianwei (Front Guard of the Garrison Militia) and Jinwu youwei (Right Guard of the Imperial Insignia Guards).

1) Military Artisans of Wugong zhongwei and Other Regional Military Units

The military artisans attached to various military units in the Hongwu era

---

[18] See *Mingshilu, Taizu shilu, juan* 195, p. 8.

[19] For information on Guo Chun, see Hou-mei Sung, "Ming Painting Academy," and "Early Ming Painters in Nanking and the Formation of the Wu School," *Ars Orientalis*, XVII, pp. 73-115.

suffered a great deal of abuse in the hands of corrupt officials and many tried to escape. In 1416 of the Yongle era, in an effort to resolve this problem, a new unit called <u>Wugong zhongwei</u> (Military Merit Center Unit) was created for the relocated or newly recruited military artisans. The new unit consists of five <u>Qianhusuo</u> (Battalions), prefixed <u>zhongzuo</u> (center-left), <u>zhongyou</u> (center-right), <u>zhongzhong</u> (center-center), <u>zhongqian</u> (center-front) and <u>zhonghou</u> (center-rear).[20] Later, in 1427 of the Xuande era, a second unit, <u>Wugong zuowei</u> (Military Merit Left Unit), of the same size was added.[21] Only one year later, in 1428, the same unit was expanded to ten Battalions. A third unit, <u>Wugong youwei</u> (Military Merit Right Unit), also containing ten Battalions, was added in 1431.[22] Artisans in these units were recruited from various military units and could be dispatched to assist with work projects in each region.

The non-military nature of these units made their position rather vague in the Ming official system. In the Yongle era, they were under the supervision of Wu Zhong, the Minister of Works.[23] But when <u>Wugong zuowei</u> was added in 1427 of the Xuande era, they were placed under the Ministry of War and supervised by officials of <u>Yülin qianwei</u>.[24]

Although military artisans of <u>Wugong zhongwei</u> served mainly as laborers for construction and military projects, skilled painters or craftsmen could be transferred to the court for special projects and even become court painters. One such example is Du Lin, who started as a military artisan in one of the <u>Wugong</u> units and was promoted to <u>Wensiyuan fushi</u> in 1485.[25]

2) Military Artisans in the Imperial Bodyguard Units

Military artisans of this category played a far more important role in the

---

[20]   See *Mingshilu, Taizong shilu, juan* 183, p. 3.
[21]   See *Mingshilu, Xüanzong shilu, juan* 28, p. 7.
[22]   Ibid., *juan* 49, p. 3 and *juan* 78, p. 5.
[23]   Ibid., *juan* 28, p. 7.
[24]   Ibid., *juan* 49, p. 3.
[25]   See *Mingshilu, Xianzong shilu, juan* 265, p. 2.

Ming Painting Academy than those in the Wugong units. They were garrisoned in and around the dynastic capital and independent of the military hierarchy.[26] Among the numerous imperial bodyguard units, three will be introduced here because of their direct associations with the Ming Painting Academy. They are Jinyiwei, Fujun qianwei and Jinwuwei. All three were nurturing grounds for the Ming court painters.

Jinyiwei

Among the various imperial bodyguard units, the earliest and most important one was Jinyiwei. Although military artisans of the Jinyiwei were first established in 1393,[27] no court painter was offered any Jinyiwei titles in the Hongwu reign. Previous research, based on available Ming painting records, typically cited Emperor Xuanzong as the first to have employed such practice, as evidenced by the Jinyiwei baihu and qianhu titles he offered to Xie Huan. However, other sources reveal that many painters, including Zhao Lian, Huang Sheng, Xü Ying, Shang Xi and Han Xiushi received Jinyiwei titles during the Yongle era.[28] Furthermore, Xü Ying received the Jinyiwei baihu (6a) title before 1417.[29] The time frame of Xü's title suggests that offering military titles to the Ming court painters was a practice started soon after the formation of the Ming Painting Academy in 1414. After the Yongle era, the military artisans of the Jinyiwei became the primary candidates for the Ming Painting Academy.

Fujun qianwei

The infiltration of military artisans into the Ming Painting Academy and the full operation of the Jinyiwei ranking system for Ming court painters can

---

[26]   See *Minghuiyao* (Beijing, Zhonghua shuju, 1956), *juan* 42, p. 749.

[27]   See *Mingshilu, Taizu shilu, juan* 227, p. 4.

[28]   For Zhao Lian, see Wang Ying, *Wang Wenangong shiji, juan* 2, p. For the other painters, see Chapter Three..

[29]   See Ye Sheng, *Shuidong riji, juan*   40, pp. 4-5.

both be traced to Xuanzong even before his enthronement. As a young child, Zhu Zhanji (future Xuanzong) had greatly impressed his grandfather, the Yongle emperor, by his wide range of interests and talents. In 1412, when Zhu Zhanji was the Imperial Grandson-heir (huangtaisun), the Yongle emperor asked Jin Zhong, the Minister of War, to recruit a group of strong and talented young men aged between seventeen and twenty to serve as special attendants of the thirteen year old grandson.[30] Three years later (1415), this youthful unit was formally designated as Fujün qianwei (Front Guard of the Garrison Militia) and placed under the supervision of qinjün zhihui shisi (Military Command of Imperial Bodyguard Units).[31] There is evidence that suggests quite a few members of this youthful unit later became leading members of the Xuande Painting Academy. At least one prominent painter of the Xuande Painting Academy, Yin Shan, can be traced to this unit.

Yin Shan was a little known painter until the recent reconstruction of his biography and the discovery of a painting by him in the tomb of Wang Zhen. It is possible to trace Yin Shan's first promotion to 1452, when he was promoted from the rank of Qianhu (Battalion Commander, 5a) to Zhihui qianshi (Assistant Commander, 4a). He reached his final rank of Zhihui tongzhi (Vice Commander, 3b) in 1459. However, for Yin Shan to climb to the high rank of Zhihui qianshi, he must have started his career in the late Yongle era (1425-1434). Also confirming Yin's early career in the Yongle court is his registration in the Fujün qianwei discussed earlier. His early relationship to Emperor Xuanzong as a talented young attendant explains the special patronage and privilege he and his son received. Both his son and grandson were able to inherit Yin Shan's high rank and status.[32]

Although insufficient biographical information on Xü Ying, Han Xiushi and Shang Xi made it impossible to trace their early career, the outstanding

---

[30] See *Mingshilu, Taizong shilu, juan* 131, p. 1.
[31] Ibid., *juan* 163, p. 1.
[32] See Hou-mei Sung, "The Three Yin Masters of the Ming Court: Yin Shan, Yin Hsieh, and Yin Hung," *Artibus Asiae*, v. LVIII, no. 1/2 (1998), pp. 91-113.

high ranks they had reached at the very beginning of the Xuande era suggest that all three had a similar early relationship with Emperor Xuanzong. The three painters' special status is clearly indicated by a comparison of their career paths with that of Xie Huan. Despite the fact that Xie was one of the most senior painters in the Xuande court, his official rank is far below those of the three cited above. In the very beginning of the Xuande era, when Xie was offered a Jinyi baihu (6a), Han Xiushi and the others was already serving as Zhihui qianshi (4a). In 1435, when Xie received his Qianhu (5a), the three masters were all promoted to Zhihui tongzhi (3b)(See biographies of the three painters in Chapter Three). In addition to superior ranks, the three leading masters also enjoyed inheritable status, a privilege reserved for merited military officials only. How did the three painters gain such superior status, unmatched by any senior members of the Yongle Academy in the beginning of the Xuande era? Considering Zhu Zhanji's early interest in painting and his close association with the group of talented youthful attendants, it is easy to understand that when he became the emperor, those who served him as imperial bodyguards or artisans would become prominent members of his Painting Academy. Since the three painters would then already have accumulated military titles, they naturally ended up higher in rank then other painters in court.

Jinwuwei

In addition to Fujün qianwei, many Ming court painters could also trace their early career to Jinwuwei (Imperial Insignia Guard). Little information is available on Jinwuwei. But judging from the careers of the three painters, Ni Duan, Liu Jün, and Zhang Ji (see Chapter Three), who all originated from this unit, Jinwuwei appears to be part of the imperial bodyguard unit of Donggong (Eastern Palace) when Zhu Jianshen (future Xianzong) was the heir apparent.

While most of the painters discussed above were recruited as military artisans to the various imperial bodyguard units based on their special talents and skills, there were also those, who gained their positions through military merits earned by their fathers or other family members. Ning Zhen, Liu Jin, and Liu Jie all belong to this category. One exceptional case is Sun Long. Although Sun entered the Xuande court through the military merits earned by his father and grandfather, he was also the descendent of a military noble. Therefore, Sun served officially as an honored imperial companion rather than a court painter (see Sun's biography in Chapter Three).

Before the Painting Academy was established, military artisans performed duties similar to their civilian counterparts in the Yingshansuo and Wensiyuan and had little prospect of improving their low status in court. But after the Jinyiwei ranking system was extended to painters, they were given a new channel to success. In fact, the access to the Jinyiwei salaries and privilege soon became the most attractive alternative for a large population of low ranking or unranked hereditary military personnel, who had little hope for a military career.

Also contributing to the surge of military artisans in the mid-Ming court was the catastrophe of Emperor Yingzong's campaign at Tumu. In August 1449, the emperor led an expedition against the northern invader, Esen. He appointed his younger brother, Zhu Qiyü (Jingdi, ruled 1450-57) to be regent and selected an entourage of a large number of military and civilian officials (totaling about half a million). The hastily prepared and poorly organized campaign soon led to a major disaster. While encamped at the post station, Tumu, the Mongols suddenly attacked. Nearly all the emperor's men were massacred and the emperor was captured.[33] During this ill-fated campaign of 1449, numerous military and civilian officials lost their lives. According to the Ming military regulation, those who died in combat or earned special military merits in war were entitled to the privilege of inheritable status. Many military artisans perished in the 1449 campaign. Thus, in the following

---

[33] See Wu Zhihe, "Tumu zhibian hou mingchao yü wala zhijiaoshe," *Mingshi yanjiu zhuankan*, v. 3, pp. 75.

Jingtai era, a large number of military personnel either inherited the positions of their fathers or gained positions as military artisans through such special military merits.

Patronage and Functions of Ming Court Painting

The relatively peaceful time from the Zhengtong (1435-1449) to the Chenghua (1465-1487) era led to further imperial patronage of the arts. However, with the dramatic changes in the Ming court painters' status, including their military artisan backgrounds and close affiliation with the eunuchs, the Ming Painting Academy was no longer an independent institution like its Song counterpart. The court painters increasingly catered to imperial needs.

From the very beginning of the Ming dynasty, the emperors took full advantage of painting as a tool for political and social gains. Even Emperor Hongwu, who considered painting superfluous, commissioned a portrait of the tribute horse from Xia as a token of his military achievement.[34] The Yongle emperor, who usurped the throne from his nephew Zhu Yünwen, relied on a large number of politically motivated paintings to justify his mandate of heaven. In addition to a scroll depicting eight of the imperial horses that died during his northern campaign to glorify his military accomplishments,[35] he also commissioned a Zhouyütu. Zhouyü was the legendary benevolent animal, which appears only when a wise ruler is presiding. The painting portrays an exotic white tiger found in Henan by Yongle's brother, Prince of Chou. Clearly, the staged appearance of the white tiger and the commissioning of its portrait were carefully calculated political events.[36]

---

[34]   See *Mingshilu, Taizu shilu, juan* 67, p. 4 and Huang Huai, *Jieanji, juan* 4, pp. 4-5, Longmage.

[35]   "The Symbolic Language of Chinese Horse Painting," *National Palace Museum Bulletin*, v. 36, no. 2 (July 2002), pp. 29-73 (cited as "Horse")

[36]   "Chinese Tiger Painting Themes and Their Symbolic Meanings, Part 2: Tiger Painting of the Yuan and Ming Dynasties," *National Palace Museum Bulletin*, v. XXXIII, no. 6 (January-February 1999), pp.

Emperor Xuanzong further widened the scope of the political and social contents of his court painting. In addition to paintings glorifying his personal achievements, like Xuanzong shelie (The Imperial Hunt of Xuanzong), he also encouraged court painters to paint historical and didactic themes, which reflected his Confucian ideals and political propaganda. Such examples include Bainiao chaofeng (Hundred Birds Worshipping Phoenix), Yingxion duojin (A Hero Claims His Trophy), Wuluntu (The Five Confucian Relationships), Zouyütu (The Auspicious White Tiger), and Congma xingchun (The Spring Tour of the Investigating Censor).[37]

Following Xuanzong, Emperor Yingzong demonstrated his interest and ability in painting when he personally painted Suihantu (Perseverance in the Wintry Season) to award the faithful service of Yü Shan.[38] Yet among all the Ming emperors, Emperor Xianzong, was perhaps the most enthusiastic patron. His fascination with using painting to convey auspicious messages is illustrated by many of his surviving paintings: Yituan heqi (All in Harmony), Suichao jiazhao (Good Omen of the New Year), Shuangxitu (Two Magpies or Double Happiness), and Dongzhi yiyangtu (One Sheep in Winter or A Ray of Sunlight in the Winter).[39] During his reign, the Ming Painting Academy reached its zenith in both the range of specialties and quality of paintings. Nevertheless, Xianzong's exceptional patronage also generated strong indignation among both civil and military officials, which eventually led to their downfall in the following Hongzhi era. In the later years of his reign, Xiaozong was pressured to eliminate a great number of court painters. Yet his appreciation of the masterpieces produced by the court painters was demonstrated when he used two of Lü Ji's paintings to educate the heir

---

33-45 (cited as "Tiger").
[37] For discussion of these themes, see Hou-mei Sung, "The Eagle Painting Themes of the Ming Court," *Archives of Asian Art*, XLVIII (1995), pp.48-63, "Horse", and "Tiger"
[38] See Yü's epitaph in Lü Yuan, *Lü Wenyi gong qüanji, juan* 10, pp. 10-13.
[39] Both Yituan heqi and Suichao jiazhao are in the collection of Beijing Palace Museum. Shuangxitu, dated 1480, is in the Jilin Provincial Museum, Damoxiang and Dongzhi yiyang, both dated 1480, are in the National Palace Museum, Taipei.

apparent.[40]

Supervision by Silijian and Yuyongjian

Although the eunuchs gained supervision of court painters as early as the late Yongle era, they did not fully exercise their power until the Chenghua era (1465-1487). Before the Chenghua era, court painters' promotions were ordered directly by the emperor. Since they followed neither the system of the civil officials, whose promotions were regulated by Libu (the Ministry of Personnel), nor that of the military officials, regulated by Bingbu (the Ministry of War), the court painters' fate and interests rested solely in the hands of the emperor. This changed when Emperor Xianzong started to delegate the duty to the powerful eunuchs of the Silijian (Directorate of Ceremonial) and Yuyongjian. As pointed out by many historians, Emperor Xianzong was mainly responsible for the abuse of chuanfeng, a procedure mainly used to promote painters and artisans. This method allowed the leading eunuch of the Silijian to transmit an imperial order to the Grand Secretariat, who then drew up a patent appointing a certain person to an office or promoting an official to a higher rank. Though existing earlier, chuanfeng was used only in rare occasions and was subjected to review by the ministers. In the Chenghua era, however, the procedure was used in alarming frequency to promote a large number of painters and artisans. This raised much controversy and touched off strong protests from both civil and military officials. Throughout the Chenghua era, chuanfeng was the single most targeted item among the endless proposals for reform.[41]

Indeed, records of the Chenghua era revealed numerous irregular promotions through the chuanfeng procedure for painters. The first one occurred in 1466, when a large number artisans and painters were promoted to

---

[40]   See Hou-mei Sung, "The Eagle Painting Themes of the Ming Court," *Archives of Asian Art*, XLVIII (1995), pp.48-63.

[41]   See *Mingshilu*, Xianzong *shilu*, *juan* 214, pp. 2-3; *juan* 247, p. 6; and *juan* 248, pp. 5-6.

Yingshan suocheng and Jinyiwei zhenfu. The promotion, although ordered by the emperor, was recommended by the eunuchs.[42] In 1470, another sixteen artisans and painters in Yuyongjian were promoted to Fushi of Wensiyuan through an edict announced by an anonymous eunuch.[43] In 1472, thirty workers participated in the renovation of Longshan temple were appointed to Fushi of Wensiyuan and some others received promotions. This caused an immediate protest from Wang Zhao, the Gongke jishizhong (Supervising Secretary of Office of Scrutiny for Works), but it was ignored by the emperor.[44] In 1473, Huang Si, a chief eunuch in Silijian, announced an imperial edict, which promoted officials in many agencies, including artisans in the Wensiyuan.[45] Starting from 1477, the frequency and scale of   promotions for painters and artisans reached new heights. In fact, from 1480 to 1487, with the exception of 1485, several announcements of promotions for painters or artisans were published almost every month and sometimes several times in a single month.[46] As a result, many painters of the Chenghua court received a promotion every three years, which was three times faster than other officials. These irregular promotions triggered numerous protests. The strongest was the organized effort in 1485. In the beginning of 1485, the astrological officials reported the disaster of a falling meteor, which was traditionally interpreted as a warning from heaven. Immediately, the three Ministers from the Ministries of Personnel, Rites, and War made a joint memorial for reform. The major issue stressed by all three was to abolish the irregular promotions of the court painters and artisans.[47] Under such strong pressure, the emperor was forced to eliminate a great number of minor artisans and painters. He also had to cancel some of the painters' titles, particularly those received through the irregular

---

[42]   Ibid., *juan* 35, p. 7.
[43]   Ibid., *juan* 84, p. 9.
[44]   Ibid., *juan* 106, p. 2.
[45]   Ibid., *juan* 122, p. 2.
[46]   Ibid., *juan* 170-293.
[47]   Ibid., *juan* 260, p. 5.

procedure and reduced some of their salaries to half. But only four months later, the emperor restored the salaries of all his court painters to the original amount.[48]

Also overlooked by most Ming historians is the great contribution of the Ming eunuchs of Silijian and Yuyongjian to the prosperity of the Ming arts. This is especially true in the Chenghua era, when the eunuchs from Silijian became more aggressive in promoting painters and artisans. The result was an era of the most productive and highest performance of all the court arts, especially painting, ceramic, and lacquer. On the other hand, the eunuchs' enthusiastic promotion of the painters soon led to the downfall of the Ming painting Academy.

While the rising power and corruption of the Ming eunuchs have been well studied by many Ming historians,[49] their direct involvement in the promotion and supervision of court painters has never been examined.

During the reigns of Yingzong and Jingdi, eunuchs climbed steadily in their political and economic power. The two most powerful eunuchs of the Zhengtong era were Ruan Lang, the chief eunuch of Yuyongjian,[50] and Jin Ying, the head eunuch in Silijian.[51] Ruan's involvement with the court painters was clearly indicated in 1457, when Yingzong was in captivity under Esen and Ruan ordered the court painter Zhao Fu to paint a Buddhist deity as a prayer for Yingzong's life (see biography of Zhao Fu). Jin Ying was more interested in painting than Ruan Lang. He was the first to recognize the talent of Zhou Qüan, a famous horse and figure painter. He later adopted Zhou as his son. Through Jin's influence, Zhou was able to serve as a military artisan in the Jinyiwei during the Zhengtong era and later reached the highest rank of

---

[48]   Ibid., *juan* 265, p. 2.

[49]   Wang Chunyü and Du Wanyan, *Mingdai huanguan yu jingji shiliao chutan* (Beijing, 1986) and Zhang Cunwu, "Shuomingdai huanguan," *Mingshi yanjiu luncong*, v. 2, p. 21.

[50]   For Ruan Lang's biography, see *Guochao xianzhenglu, juan* 117, pp. 5-6.

[51]   For Jin Ying's biography, see *Guochao xianzhenglu, juan* 117, p. 10, *Mingren zhuanji ziliao suoyin*, p, 308 and *Dictionary of Ming Biography*, pp. 246-247.

Zhihui.

Crucial to the mid-Ming court painters' careers was the group of leading eunuchs of the Silijian. They include Tan Chang (1433-1495),[52] Li Rong (active 1470-80)[53], Xiao Jing (1438-1528),[54] Huai En (1420's-1488),[55] and Wei Tai (died 1500).[56] Tan Chang and Li Rong were active before in the late 1470s. Xiao Jing and Huai En were involved only from 1483 to 1484. After 1485, Wei Tai, the chief eunuch of Silijian in the Hongzhi reign, became the most important advocate for court painters. Wei's active patronage of painters was also apparent through his collection of paintings by those he promoted. Two surviving paintings with Wei's seals are Zhou Qüan's Shezhitu (Shooting Pheasants)[57] and Yin Xie's Yingji tiane (A Hawk Stalking A Swan).[58]

The Decline (Hongzhi to Zhengde Eras)

Even before Emperor Xiaozong officially began his rule, an active campaign of the court officials against the chuanfeng procedure and the irregular promotion of artisans and painters was already in place. In the ninth month of 1487, memorials for reform were pouring in. In the following month, officials from both the Ministry of Personnel and Ministry of War proposed to reduce the "redundant personnel." Following the proposals was a list, which included many court painters who gained their positions through the illegitimate channel of chuanfeng. Thus, like Xianzong, Xiaozong was also pressured to eliminate a great number of court painters. The remaining painters suffered a systematic demotion. Those holding the rank level tow

---

[52] For Tan Chang's biography, see *Mingren zhuanji ziliao suoyin*, p. 637.
[53] Li Rong's biography is not found among any Ming records.
[54] Xiao Jing's biography, see *Mingren zhuanji ziliao suoyin*, p. 908.
[55] Ibid., p. 933.
[56] Wei Tai was active in the late Chenghua era and served as the Taijian of Silijian.
[57] The painting is in the collection of the National Palace Museum, Taipei. See *Gugong shuhualu, juan* 5, p.
[58] For discussion of Yin's Yingji tiane in Nanking Museum, see Hou-mei Sung, "The Three Yin Masters of the Ming Court: Yin Shan, Yin Hsieh, and Yin Hung," *Artibus Asiae*, v. LVIII, no. 1/2 (1998), pp. 91-113.

were demoted to a <u>Zhengqianhu</u> (5a), rank level three to a <u>Fuqianhu</u> (5b), rank level four to a <u>Baihu</u> (6a), and rank level five to <u>Guandai zongqi</u> (unranked, Platoon Commander), and rank level six to a <u>Guandai xiaoqi</u> (Squad Commander). However, those who gained their position because of special merit, or due to inherited military merit, would still be recognized as creditable. They would lose only the titles gained through the <u>chuanfeng</u> procedure. The proposed reform was carried out in the following month.[59]

The campaign against the artisans and court painters did not stop after the reform of 1487. In 1491, citing the appearance of a comet in 1490 as a warning from heaven, high officials again proposed to reduce the number of court painters and artisans, especially those with high military ranks. Since then, the officials carefully guarded against any further promotion of artisans or painters. Given the increasing tension between the officials and the eunuchs who supervised the artisans and painters, it is not surprising that another announcement of irregular promotion for artisans and painters immediately touched off a new wave of strong protests. It happened in the seventh month of 1494, when Wei Tai, the leading eunuch of <u>Silijian,</u> carried out the imperial order to promote four senior painters, including Zhang Ji and thirty artisans.[60] The promotion was indeed irregular, because all of them were raised two ranks instead of one. But its intent was to compensate those painters who suffered demotion in 1487 (see Zhang Ji's biography). In the same month, Geng Yü, the Minister of Personnel also submitted a memorial to the emperor urging him to cancel the ranks. Shortly after this, Zhou Xüan, the <u>Jishizhong</u> (Supervising Secretary) of <u>Bingke</u> (Office of Scrutiny for War) submitted his memorial condemning the abuse of the military ranks. Zhou repeated the same message in another memorial two months later. Many others also joined the protest.[61] The emperor did not change his decision, but the irregular and

---

[59] See *Ming Shilu, Xiaozong shilu,   juan* 2, pp. 11-13, *juan* 3, p. 1, 8, and *juan* 4, p. 1- 2.
[60] Ibid., *juan* 90, p. 4,
[61] Ibid., *juan* 90 p. 6,   *juan* 91, p. 3;   *juan* 92, p. 2; *juan* 94, p. 4; *juan* 95, pp. 1-2; *juan* 99, p. 7; *juan*

frequent promotion of painters through the chuanfeng procedure was sharply reduced after this.

Other than targeting the existing painters and artisans, efforts were also made to curb new recruits. In the eleventh month of 1494, Chai Sheng, the Youjishizhong (Right Supervising Secretary) of Gongke (Office of Scrutiny for Works), remonstrated against the emperor's efforts to recruit painters from Shanxi and Shandong provinces and suggested that the emperor cancel the whole project. Emperor Xiaozong responded by stating that he would take care of the matter when the painters arrived at the capital. Unsatisfied with this response, Wei Chun, the Bingke jishizhong (Supervising Secretary of Office of Scrutiny for War), repeated the same message one month later. Citing the recent natural disasters as warnings from heaven, Wu advised the emperor to halt recruiting any more painters and send back those already arrived.[62] From 1499 to 1505, more memorials arrived proposing further reduction or total elimination of the court painters.[63] Although the emperor continued to patronize his court painters till the end of his reign, the chuanfeng procedure was never used again.

In 1505, as soon as Emperor Wuzong ascended the throne, he immediately carried out the proposed measures for reform and eliminated 224 low ranked artisans and court painters. All the titles gained through the chuanfeng procedure were cancelled and those who remained suffered another round of systematic reduction of salary and rank demotion similar to that of 1487.[64] This signified a major set back for all court painters, including Ni Duan, Lü Wenying, Wang E, and Yuan Lin, Zhu Duan and Zhao Linsu.

The canceling of the Ming court painters' ranks in 1487 and 1505 has

---

102, p. 2; and *juan* 111, p. 5.
[62] Ibid., *juan* 91, p. 3; *juan* 92, p. 2 ; *juan* 94, p. 4; and *juan* 95, pp. 1-2
[63] Ibid., *juan* 155, pp. 6-7; *juan* 157, p. 1, pp. 3- 4 and p. 10; *juan* 159, p. 6; *juan* 160, p. 6; *juan* 162, p. 9; *juan* 164, p. 10; *juan* 165, p. 7; *juan* 175, pp. 6-7; *juan* 178, p. 4; *juan* 188, p. 5; *juan* 198, p. 3; *juan*   211, p. 5, and *juan* 211, p. 11
[64] *Wuzong shilu, juan* 10, p. 15; *juan* 12, p. 1; *juan* 85, p. 6 and *juan* 88, p. 4

caused a great deal of confusion for later art historians. Many painters continued to sign their works with the higher ranks gained before the reduction or cancellation. Some specified their official title by adding a prefix. For instance, in *Jiaxing fuzhi,* Zhu Duan and Zhao Linsu were recorded as "shizhihuifeng" (serving the salary rank of a Jinyi zhihui) and "shou Jinyiwei fuqianhufeng" (serving the salary rank of a Jinyiwei fuqianhu).[65] In other words, after the Zhengde reform, court painters no longer received the honorary Jinyiwei titles, only their equivalent salaries. This also meant that they could no longer enjoy the privileges of inheriting titles or climbing to high ranks. In this increasingly hostile environment, painters were discouraged from seeking service inside the court and the Painting Academy slowly faded away.

---

[65]   See Mu Yiqin, *Mingdai yuanti zhepai shiliao,* p. 63.

Chapter Three

Ming Court Painters: Military and Civilian Artisan Painters

Much of our new knowledge on the history, unique structure, and operation of the Ming Painting Academy comes from the biographical information of the Ming court painters. Instrumental to our understanding of the ranking system of the Ming court painters are the diverse social backgrounds and career paths of the military and civilian artisan painters. After a long investigation, I have reconstructed the biographies of a group of Ming court painters, who were either previously unrecorded or poorly represented in our account of Ming painting history. While some have no surviving paintings to represent their achievements, all played a part in the evolving Ming Painting Academy. However, the painters included here are far from a complete list of the Ming court painters, nor are their biographies comprehensive.

In addition to providing specific examples and detailed information about the operation and promotion system of the Ming Painting Academy, these biographies also help to illustrate the dichotomous career paths of the military artisan painters and the civilian painters. Since the lineage of the military artisan painters can be traced to encompass an impressive range of privileged groups, including families of military nobles and imperial guard units, they were typically admitted to the Painting Academy through imperial favors.

Some inherited their positions through the military merits of their fathers. This extensive military heritage explains not only why the military ranking system was employed in the Ming Painting Academy, but also why some Ming court painters enjoyed exceptionally high ranks and privileges.

Court Painters with Military Artisan Background

Guo Chun

Guo Chun, originally known as Guo Wentong, was recommended by Huang Huai to serve in the court in 1405. He served over ten years in the court without receiving any official title. Yet in 1414, when the Yongle emperor incidentally saw one of Guo's works, he was so impressed that he immediately summoned Guo and honored him with a new name, Chun, and the title of Yingshansuo cheng (7a). In 1424, Emperor Renzong granted him the honorary title of Gemengshi (Audience Attendant 6a) and assigned him to Xihuameng (Xihua Gate) as a Daizhao (painter-in-attendance). In 1426, Emperor Xuanzong released him from the military registration and raised his official rank to 5a. Guo retired in 1435.[66]

Han Xiushi and Shang Xi

No information is available on the origin or early career of Han Xiushi and Shang Xi, but their outstanding high ranks and special privileges in the Xuande court suggest that both had an early relationship with Emperor Xuanzong. Since the two artists shared an almost identical career path, they will be discussed together here.

Han started his service as a military artisan in the Yüyongsi (Directorate for Imperial Accoutrements) in the Yongle era (1403-1424). It is very likely that he was selected to be a member of the imperial guard unit of Fujün qianwei in the Yongle era because of his artistic talent. By the end of the

---

Yongle era, he had already climbed to the high rank of Jinyiwei zhengqianhu (5a). In 1425, Han received the promotion from Zhengqianhu (5a) to Zhihui qianshi (4a).[67] Shortly after the Xüande era (1426-1435), Han and his colleague Shang Xi were punished for some unknown offense and temporarily expelled from their positions. After a period of menial labor, both recovered their titles in the fifth month of 1430.[68] In 1435, Han and Shang were both promoted to their final title, Zhihui tongzhi (3b).[69] Han died in 1443 and his son, Yong, inherited his position. Based on the above information, Han's dates can be estimated as between the late 1380s and 1443.[70]

Shang Xi, a native of Shaoxing (Zhejiang), shared with Han Xiushi all the dated promotions cited above. Shang died around 1450, and his son Ying inherited his title.[71] Both Han and Shang were known for a great variety of subjects. Today, Han's only attributed work is a pair of hanging scrolls depicting carp. Shang's extant works include paintings of figures, horses, cats, and flowers-and-birds.

Xü Ying and Xü Lin

Xü Ying and his son, Lin, are little known painters in Ming painting history. Yet Xu Ying's position as a leading Ming court painter is revealed by the following event recorded by Yuan Zhongzhe (1376-1458):

"On the 18th of the fifth month of 1417, the Yongle emperor asked (Yuan) Zhongzhe and Xü Ying, the court painter of the Baihu rank, to join him in viewing the portraits of the Song emperors."[72]

---

[67] See *Xuande Shilu* in *Mingshilu, juan* 9, p. 16.
[68] See *Xuande Shilu* in *Mingshilu, juan* 66, p. 3.
[69] See *Yingzong Shilu* in *Mingshilu, juan* 11, p. 4.
[70] See Hou-mei Sung, "Chinese Fish Painting and Its Symbolic Meanings: Fish Painting of the Ming Dynasty," *National Palace Museum Bulletin*, v. XXX, no. 3-4 (July-August and September-October, 1995)(quoted as "Ming Fish").
[71] See *Mingshilu, Yingzong shilu, juan* 190, p. 11.
[72] See Ye Sheng, *Shuidong riji, juan* 40, pp. 378-380.

As Yuan pointed out, in 1417 Xü Ying was serving as a <u>Baihu</u>. Xü must have received a <u>Qianhu</u> title later in the Yongle era, because in 1425, he was promoted from <u>Qianhu</u> to <u>Zhihui qianshi</u> (4a). It is not clear when Xü retired. But, in 1435, when Emperor Yingzong came to the throne, Ying was summoned to the court again and offered to the higher rank of <u>Zhihui tongzhi</u> (3b). Ying requested that the emperor transfer the higher title to his son, Lin, while he continued to serve under his former title, <u>Zhihui qianshi</u> (4a), and was granted this favor.[73]

Although Xü Ying's background is not clear, judging from his high ranks and the fact that he was allowed to transfer his high rank to his son even during his lifetime, he was likely connected to either a prominent military noble or a privileged imperial guard unit. Xü's exceptional reputation is evident when one compares Xü's case with that of Huang Sheng, another unrecorded painter in the Xüande court. In 1429, when Huang, a court painter of the <u>Baihu</u> rank, is ready for retirement, he made a similar plea to the emperor for his son to replace him with the same rank and was bluntly refused.[74]

Sun Long

Sun Long[75] was the grandson of Sun Xingzu (1338-1370), a chief military aid for Emperor Hongwu. Sun Xingzu died in a major battle in 1370 at the age of thirty-three and was honored with the noble title of <u>Yanshanhou</u> (Commandant of Yanshan).[76] As the grandson of a military noble, Sun Long was entitled to inherit military ranks of his father, Sun Ke. Unfortunately, in an effort to purge the powerful military nobility, the Hongwu emperor stripped

---

[73] See *Mingshilu, Yingzong shilu, juan* 11, p. 6.

[74] See *Mingshilu, Xüanzong shilu, juan* 56, p. 2.

[75] For the confusion of the biographies of the two Sun Long in the early Ming era, see see Xü Banda, "Sun Long he Sun Long Kaobian," *Gugong bowuyuan yuankan*, (1982), no. 4, pp. 22-24 and Xüe Yongnian, "Sün Long di liangjian zhenji jiqi yishu," *Gugong bowuyuan yuankan*, (1981), no. 1, pp. 38-42.

[76] For Sun Xingzu's biography, see *Mingren zhuanji ziliao suoyin*, p. 442.

Sun Ke of his military title and power. So, instead of inheriting the family's military career and privileges, Sun Long was recognized by his talent as a painter and was invited to the court as Xuanzong's special companion. There are indications that Sun not only joined Xuanzong in painting, but also assisted in some of the emperor's paintings. Some of Xuanzong's paintings indeed possess the same spontaneous "boneless" style of Sun. It was common practice for the descendants of the Ming founding heroes to serve as special attendants of the emperor (Sheren). Sun's seal, "Jinmen Shiyü" (Attending the Emperor at the Golden Gates), which frequently appeared on his paintings, also confirmed such a position. It is therefore necessary to distinguish Sun from a regular court painter. Sun's seal, "Jinmen Shiyü," should not be confused with a similar seal used by many other Ming court painters, "Jinmen huashi" (Court painters of the Golden Gates). Thus, although Sun served in the Xuande court in the capacity of a painter, he was not a member of the Painting Academy.

Ning Zheng

Ning Zheng is not listed in any Ming painting records as a painter, but according to Lü Yuan (1418-1462), "Few painters in the court can exceed his skill." Ning came from a military family of great merits. Both his grandfather Ning Zheng and father Ning Zhong served as Jinyiwei zhihui in the Hongwu and Yongle eras and both died on duty. Because of this birthright, Zheng was granted the position of a military artisan in the Jinyiwei. In 1454, he was promoted to Jinyiwei suozhenfu (6b).[77]

Zhang Jing

Biographical sources on Ming painters provide us with little information on Zhang other than that he was a figure painter from Shangdong. Yet new

---

[77]   Ning Zhen's biography is based on *Mingshilu, Taizu shilu, juan* 245, p. 6; *Yingzong shilu, juan* 246, p. 1; and Lü Yuan, *Lüwenyi gongwenji, juan* 8, p. 10.

evidence reveals that Zhang started his career by serving in the Yuyongjian as a military artisan of the Jinyiwei. In 1456, he was promoted to the rank of Zhengqianhu (5a) and became a leading painter in court. However, in 1485, for some unknown reason, Zhang was demoted to the low rank of Dashi (9a) of Wensiyuan.[78]

Zhang Ji and Zhang Jin

Zhang Ji was the son of Zhang Bao, who served as Zhihhui jianshi (4a) in the imperial guard unit of Jinwu zuowei (Imperial Insignia Guard, Left Division). Zhang Ji inherited his father's title in 1457 and was moved to Jinyiwei as a court painter. As the son of a high military official, Zhang was differentiated from the regular military artisans as a guanjiang, which entitled him to many military privileges. In 1477, he was promoted from Zhihui qianshi to Zhihui tongzhi (3b). In 1480, he became a Duzhihui qianshi and again, in 1482, a Duzhihui tongzhi. Finally in 1485, Zhang Ji reached the highest rank, Duzhihuishi. The frequent and irregular promotions of Zhang and others to the high military ranks raised numerous protests and, in 1487, the emperor was pressured to demote all the court painters, including Zhang, who was demoted to a Qianhu. However, in 1494, Zhang was fully compensated when he was awarded a title two ranks higher. The irregular promotion again triggered strong protests. However, Zhang kept the title of Jinyi zhihui tongzhi and served until 1499, when his son, Jin, replaced him, also holding the same position. Zhang Jin's career as a court painter started earlier in 1480, when he received the title of Jinyi zhenfu. He gained the inheritable status of a Fuqianhu in 1486 and inherited his father's position of a Jinyi zhihui tongzhi in 1499.[79]

---

[78] See *Minghualu, juan* 1, p. 4; *Wusheng shishi, juan* 6, p. 98; *Yingzoung shilu*, v. 267, p. 2; and *Xianzong shihlu*, v. 265, p. 2.

[79] Zhang Ji was mistaken as the son of Zhang Jing in *Zhongguo meishu jiarenming cidian* (pp. 827-828). For the dates and career of Zhang Ji and Zhang Jin, see *Yingzong shilu, juan* 280, p. 13; *Xianzong shilu, juan* 170, p. 6, *juan* 208, p. 5, *juan* 229, p. 6, *juan* 265, p. 6, and *Xiaozong shilu, juan*

Liu Jin and Liu Jie

Liu Jin and his son, Liu Jie, are two dominant figures in the mid-Ming court. Their dedication to fish painting raised the subject to a new height in both its popularity and its originality. However, as is typical of the Ming court painters, little is known about the two Liu masters.

The Liu family came from Ancheng, Jiangxi. At the beginning of the Ming era, the family was registered as a member of the military unit in Fuyü of Rehe province. After the Yongle era, when the Fuyü unit was abolished, the family transferred to Beijing. In 1449 of the Zhengtong era, Liu Xin, grandfather of Liu Jie, participated in the emperor's campaign against Esen and died during the disastrous fight at the post station of Tumu. Liu Xin's son, Jin, then inherited his father's place in the military service as a military artisan. In the autumn of 1459, Jin was promoted from a military artisan to Shibaihu (acting Platoon Commander) and served as a painter in Yuyongjian (Directorate for Imperial Accouterments). Jin became well known for his fish paintings and was eventually promoted to the high rank of Jinyi zhihui (Commander of the Embroidered Uniformed Guard) during the Chenghua era (1465-1487). Based on the above information, Liu Jin's dates can be estimated as between the 1430's and the 1480's. The date of Liu Jin's death can be further narrowed to between 1481 and 1485, based on dates and information on Liu Jie's titles.[80]

Because of Liu Xin's death in the combat of 1449, the family earned the privilege of an inheritable status. Thus Liu Jin's son, Jie, also entered the court and served as a court painter sometime during the Chenghua era (1465-87). Liu Jie received his first title, Wensiyüan fushi (Vice Commissioner of the

---

90, p. 4, *juan* 91, p. 3, *juan* 92, p. 2, *juan* 155, p. 9, *juan* 157, p. 10, *juan* 208, p. 5.

[80]   See Hou-mei Sung, "Chinese Fish Painting of the Sung and Yuan Dynasties and Its Symbolic Meanings," *National Palace Museum Bulletin*, v. XXX, no. 1 & 2 (May-June, 1995), p. 1 and "Chinese Fish Painting of the Ming Dynasty and Its Symbolic Meanings," *National Palace Museum Bulletin*, v. XXX, no. 3 & 4 (July-August, September-October, 1995), p. 1.

Crafts Institute) in 1477 through the recommendation of the eunuch, Tan Chang. In the autumn of 1480, Liu Jie was promoted to Wensiyüan dashi (Commissioner-in-chief) of the Crafts Institute through eunuch Li Rong. His next promotion was not recorded, yet by 1485 Liu Jie was already a Zhihui qianshi. Since it is impossible that Liu might have climbed five ranks within five years, it is likely that Liu's father, Jin, died sometime between 1481 and 1485 and Liu Jie then inherited his father's rank. Unfortunately, in the first month of 1485, Liu Jie and most of the other senior painters in court, suffered a temporary set back in their careers when the astrological officials sighted a falling meteor and interpreted it as a warning from heaven. Among the proposed reforms to the government was to abolish the honorary military titles offered to court painters and to eliminate the many "useless" painters in court. Under the pressure, the emperor reduced a great number of minor artisans and painters. For the remaining court painters, Liu Jie among them, their salaries were reduced by half. Four months later, in the summer of 1485, Liu's salary was restored to the original amount. In 1486, Liu Jie was granted the imperial favor allowing his son to inherit the title of Fuqianhu (Vice Battalion Commander). No information is available after 1486, yet Liu was probably promoted to his final rank of Jinyi zhihui in the early Hongzhi era. Based on the above information, Liu Jie's dates can be estimated as between the 1450's to 1510's.

Ni Duan

According to *Minghualu*, Ni first entered the court during the Xüande era (1426-35). This seems unlikely considering he was still active in court in the early Hongzhi era (1488 - 1505). It is more likely that Ni served from the Zhengtong era (1436-1449) to the Hongzhi era and was most active in the Chenghua era. New evidence also indicates that Ni's military background can be traced to Jinwu youwei (Imperial Insignia Guard, Right Division), a distinguished unit of the imperial bodyguard, which was likely a unit in the

Donggong (Eastern Palace), the designated residence of the heir apparent. Although no specific date is given, judging from his rapid promotion and favorable patronage during the Chenghua era, his service in the Donggong was likely during the reign of Zhengtong, when Emperor Xianzong was heir apparent. Ni's close affiliation with the heir-apparent must have helped his career as a court painter. In 1456, the seventh year of the Jingtai era, he had already climbed to the rank of Baihu. His subsequent promotions were not clearly recorded. It is probable that he received his second promotion in 1459. According to the palace record, in that year nine court painters serving the Baihu rank received their promotions to the next rank of Qianhu. Ni must have been promoted once again, before 1480, to the rank of Zhihui qianshi (4a), because the next record shows his final promotion from a Jinyi zhihui tongzhi (3b) to the highest rank of Duzhihuishi (3a) in 1480. After reaching the highest position, he continued to benefit from imperial favors. For instance, in the twelfth month of 1485, he was given four assistants and in the second month of 1486, another four were added. After Emperor Xianzong died in September of 1486, Ni suffered a temporary setback because of the strong protests by court officials. In the tenth month of 1487, he was demoted to Zhihui qianshi (4a) and ordered to return to his original unit of Jinwu youwei. However, within one year, in December 1488, Emperor Xiaozong granted him permission to return to the Jinyiwei. In 1505, when Emperor Wuzong came to the throne, Ni was again targeted and affected by a major reform carried out that year. However, no details are available as to how Ni's ranks or salaries were adjusted.

The two extant paintings by Ni, Pinpangtu in Beijing Palace Museum and Buyūtu in National Palace Museum, Taipei, confirm his reputation as a master of both figure and landscape. The Taipei work contains his official seals, "Jinyi qianhu zhizhang." With the reconstructed biography above, it is now possible to date the painting to shortly after the year 1459, when Ni received his Jinyi qianhu title.[81]

Yin Shan, Yin Xie, Yin Shun, and Yin Hong

The reconstructed biographies of Yin Shan, Yin Xie, Yin Shun and Yin Hong have been included in an earlier publication and will only be summarized here.[82]

Yin Shan (ca.1410s to 1460s) came from a military family registered in the imperial guard unit of Fujun qianwei. His career very likely started in the Xuande (1425-1434) era. This can be deduced from the fact that he was promoted from the rank of Qianhu (Battalion Commander, 5a) to Zhihui qianshi (Assistant Commander, 4a) in 1452, the third year of Jingtai reign (1450-1457). Before the Zhengtong era (1436-1449), the promotion of court painters followed the regulation of upgrading once every nine years. Therefore, for Yin to be promoted to the Qianhu title in the Jingtai era, he must have served more than twenty years in court. Yin's next promotion came in 1459, when he was promoted from Zhihui qianshi to his final rank of Zhihui tongzhi (Vice Commander, 3b). Although it is recorded that Yin received the 1459 promotion because he had fulfilled the requisite nine years service in the previous position, actually only seven years had passed since his 1452 promotion. A possible explanation for the discrepancy is: Yin Shan's first promotion was delayed for two years because of the chaotic circumstances surrounding Emperor Yingzong's capture by the Oirat chieftain, Esen. However, Yin Shan served only one year in his final rank. In 1460, he requested that the emperor let his son, Xie, replace him and inherit his title. The Ministry of War and others voiced their disapproval, stating that Yin Shan's request would violate the rules governing hereditary military titles. The

---

[81]   The reconstructed biography of Ni are based on *Mingshilu, Yingzong shilu, juan* 267, p. 2; *juan* 305, p. 2; *Xianzong shilu, juan* 208, p. 5; *juan.* 262, p. 2; *juan* 273, p. 2; *juan* 275, p. 4, and *Xiaozong shilu, juan* 21, p. 7. For Ni Duan's Pingpangtu, see *Mingdai gongting yü zhepai huihua xüanji*, pl.15.

[82]   See Hou-mei Sung, "The Three Yin Masters of the Ming Court: Yin Shan, Yin Hsieh, and Yin Hung," *Artibus Asiae*, v. LVIII, no. 1/2 (1998), pp. 91-113.

emperor, however, ordered the Ministry to make an exception in this case and granted Yin Shan's wish. Based upon the preceding information, Yin Shan probably was active from the late 1410s to the 1460s.

Yin Xie enjoyed a short cut in his career in 1460, when Emperor Xianzong granted Yin Shan's wish and allowed Xie to inherit his father's rank of Zhihui tongzhi. However, because of this irregular advancement, Yin Xie received no further promotion for twenty years. It was not until 1480, that he gained a prefix to his title and became a Duzhihui tongzhi, indicating his seniority but changing neither his rank nor his salary. In 1499, he was granted a transfer from the imperial guard unit of Fujün qianwei to the more prestigious Jinyiwei and the privilege of an inheritable status. Yin served until 1504, when he retired and was replaced by his son, Hong.

Yin Shun is not listed in any biographical records for Ming painters. However, newly uncovered information about his dates and his position at court suggests that he was very likely a younger brother or a cousin of Yin Xie. Yin Shun entered the court around the same time as Xie, in the 1450s. His first recorded promotion was in 1480, when he was promoted from Baihu to Qianhu. Yin Shun must have received further promotions, because by the beginning of 1485, he had already attained the rank of Zhihui qianshi (4a). Like Yin Xie, he also suffered the temporary salary cut in 1485. The following year, the emperor awarded Yin Shun an inheritable status of Fuqianhu. Although none of his paintings survives today, the senior rank Yin Shun achieved suggests that he must have been a highly accomplished painter. Also, two of Yin Shun's bird paintings were in the collection of Yan Song (1480-1565).

In 1504, Yin Hong succeeded his father as a court painter. However, due to strong protests from the Ministry of War, he did not inherit his father's rank of Zhihui tongzhi. Instead, he received the lower title of Baihu. Yin Hong's career was doomed from the beginning because he entered the court near the end of the Hongzhi era, when the strong imperial patronage for court painters was under severe and repeated attacks from both civil and military officials. The eunuchs, who served as supervisors for the court painters, were also losing power. In the succeeding Zhengde reign, court painters suffered a further setback when a large number of them were dismissed and the remaining members received major reductions in ranks, salaries, and privileges. Yin Hong was never promoted to a rank higher than the one he inherited.

Liu Jün

Liu Jün came from a military official family registered in the Jinwuwei (Imperial Insignia Guard). In the Chenghua era, Liu received many irregular promotions and advanced from a Baihu (6a) to Zhihui tongzhi (3b). However, in the beginning of 1485, Liu also suffered a demotion to Duzhihui qianshi (4a), which he held until the end of his career.[83]

Zhou Qüan

Little is known of Zhou's origin other than that he came from a military-artisan background and was adopted by Jin Ying (fl. 1425-50), the powerful eunuch serving in the early Ming court. As the head of the Silijian in the Xüande era, Jin must have recognized Zhou's talent and recommended him to the Yuyongjian.   In 1456, Zhou was promoted to the rank of Jinyi baihu through some unknown military merit (jüngong). However, shortly after this, Zhou was involved in some unknown misconduct. He was demoted to the low status of Xiaoqi (Squad Commander) and was sent to remote frontiers. He was pardoned somehow, and rose again to the rank of Qianhu sometime before 1480. In that year, he was promoted from Qianhu to Duzhihui qianshi. In 1486, Zhou received a final favor from the emperor, which would allow his heir to inherit the rank of Fuqianhu. Zhou died in the

---

[83]   See Hou-mei Sung, "Liu Jün and His Figure Painting." *Oriental Art,* v, XLV, no. 3 (1999), pp. 65 -78.

seventh month of 1487 and his nephew, Guang, inherited Qüan's former title, Jinyi zhihui qianshi.[84]

Zhao Fu

Zhao Fu was another unrecorded painter of the Ming court. He started his service in court as a military artisan of the Jinyiwei, probably in the Zhengtong era. An account of Zhao's early career was documented in the palace record of Yingzong. According to this record dated 1457, Zhao claimed that in the Jingtai era, Ruan Lang, the Vice-Director of Yuyongjian, ordered him to paint an image of a deity in order to pray for the longevity of Yingzong, who was then living like a prisoner in Nancheng after being sent back to China by Esen. Although Zhao failed to gain any reward from this claim, it probably won him a favorable impression from the emperor for both himself and Ruan Lang. The next recorded promotion of Zhao was in the tenth month of 1480, when he was promoted from a Baihu to a Qianhu. In less than two years, in the seventh month of 1482, he was again promoted to the rank of Zhihui qianshi (4a). In 1486, he was awarded two assistant clerks.[85] No further information is known of Zhao after 1486. A single painting by Zhao depicting goats and sheep is found in the collection of the Tokyo National Museum.

Ming Court Painters with Civilian-Artisan or Unknown Background

Although many Ming court painters of civilian-artisan background were also awarded the honorary Jinyiwei titles, they typically received lower ranks and had fewer privileges than their military counterparts.

---

[84] See *Yingzong shilu, juan.* 267, p. 2; *Xianzong shilu, juan* 208, p. 5; *juan* 265, p. 2, *juan* 275, p. 4, and *juan* 292, p. 1.

[85] See *Yingzong shilu. juan* 279, p. 2; *Xianzong shilu, juan* 208, p. 5; *juan* 229, p. 6; *juan* 262, p. 2; *juan* 265, p. 2; and *juan* 275, p. 4.

Bian Wenjin (ca. 1356-1428)

Bian Wenjin, a painter from Shaxian, Fujian, entered the court in the early Yongle era. He first served in the <u>Wensiyuan</u> (Craft Institutie). Although mainly known as a flower-and-bird painter, Bian also painted fish, horses, cats, architecture and landscape. Bian's outstanding talent was fully recognized even before the informal Painting Academy was established. His bird painting was considered one of the "Three Perfections of the Yongle Palace" (Jinzhong sanjue). In the early stage of his career, Bian enjoyed strong patronage from many scholar officials in the <u>Hanlin</u> Academy, including Huang Huai, Yang Rong, Zhang Ning and Lin Huan. He even collaborated with the scholar painter, Wang Fu, who served as a <u>Zhongshu sheren</u> (Secretariat Drafter). However, the status of Bian quickly changed in 1414, when the emperor placed all court painters under the eunuch controlled <u>Yuyongjian</u> (Directorate for Imperial Accoutrements). While this move laid the initial foundation of the Ming Painting Academy, it also led to an unanticipated development -- the infiltration of the military artisans to the Painting Academy in the Xuande era. Bian continued to serve in the court of Renzong (1424-1425) and Xuanzong (1426-1434). However, shortly after the Xuande era, in Jan 1427, he was accused of taking bribes and stripped of his official title. Considering Xuanzong's reorganization of the Painting Academy and his promotion of many military artisan painters serving him in the Eastern Palace (Donggong), it would not be surprising that Bian became a victim of jealousy and treachery.[86]

Xie Huan

Xie Huan came from a prominent family of scholars in Yongjia, Zhejiang. Entering the court at the beginning of Yongle era, he soon became

---

[86]   See Hou-mei Sung, "Bian Wenjin and His Flower-and-bird Painting," *Oriental Art,* v. XXXVIII, no. 3 (autumn 1992), pp. 154-164.

the leading painter. His scholarly background won him strong patronage from the scholar officials, especially Huang Huai, the Grand Secretary from his hometown. This is evidenced by his participation in the literary gathering at Xingyuan (Apricot Garden).[87] In the Xuande era, when the emperor was personally interested in painting, Xie became a favorite companion and trusted advisor. He received his <u>Baihu</u> title in 1426 and <u>Qianhu</u> in 1435. He reached his final rank of <u>Zhihui qianshi</u> in 1452. It is interesting to point out here that through the writings of the early Ming scholars one may gain the impression that Xie Huan was the most prominent member in the Xuande court, since he was one of the very few cited as having received the titles of <u>Baihu</u> and <u>Qianhu</u>. However, in reality, Xie was lower in rank than his contemporaries, Shang Xi, Han Xiushi and Xü Ying. This is demonstrated by the fact that, in 1435, when Xie received his title of <u>Jinyiwei qianhu</u> (5a), Shang Xi, Han Xiushi, and Xü Ying were also promoted to <u>Zhihui tongzhi</u> (3b). Xie did not receive his final promotion to <u>Zhihui qianshi</u> (4a) until seventeen years later in 1452 of the Jingtai era.

Shangguan Boda

Shangguan was known for paintings of many subjects, including Buddhist and Daoist figures, landscape and flower-and-bird. In the beginning of 1421, when construction of the new palace in Beijing was completed, he was summoned to serve in the hall of <u>Renzhidian</u>, where the new Painting Academy was located. After arriving in court, Shangguan presented his masterpiece, <u>Bainiao chaofeng</u> (Hundred Birds Worshipping the Phoenix), to the Yongle emperor and excused himself because of his old age. The emperor

---

[87]   See Hou-mei Sung, "From the Min-Che Tradition to the Che School, Part I: The Late Yuan Min-Che Tradition (Chang Shun-tzu and Ch'en Shu-ch'i)," *National Palace Museum Research Quarterly*, v. 6, no. 4 (1989), p. 1 and "From the Min-Che Tradition to the Che School, Part II: Precursors of the Che School (Hsieh Huan and Tai Chin," *National Palace Museum Research Quarterly*, v. 7, no. 1 (1989), p. 127.

rewarded him with gifts and granted his wish.[88]

Zhao Lian

According to *Minghualu,* Zhao was a tiger painter from Wuxing (Zhejiang) and nicknamed "Zhao Hu (Tiger Zhao)."[89] Neither his dates, nor his official status was recorded, but Zhao's talent did not go unrecognized during his lifetime. His tiger paintings were considered one of the "Three Perfections of the Imperial Palace" (Jinzhong sanjüe) at the Yongle court (the other two being bird paintings by Bian Wenjin and bodhisattvas by Jiang Zicheng).[90] Zhao, known also for dragon painting,[91] was one of the very few Yongle painters to have received the honorary military rank of Jinyiwei Baihu (Platoon Commander of the Embroidered Uniform Guard, 6a).[92]

Fang Changling

Fang came from a very different background than that of most other court painters. He was the son of Fang Liangbi, an Instructor of the National University (Guozi xuezheng). Therefore, Fang received a good classical education and showed great talent both as a scholar and painter. In his early youth, he joined his father in Beijing and his talents became widely known. In 1407, he was recommended to serve as a painter in court. However, despite his aptitude in a wide range of subjects, including figures, fish, insects, plants, Fang was forced to give up his true interest and calling. For the promising son of a scholar official to pursue the career of a court painter was considered a disgrace to the family. Fang was also alienated because of his different social background. So, after serving for a few years, he finally left the court (before 1413) on the excuse of his mother's old age and returned home in the late

---

[88] See *Shaowu fuzhi* (Jiajing ed.), *juan* 61, pp. 12-13.
[89] See Xü Xin, *Minghualu, juan* 5, p. 71.
[90] See *Jiangnan tongzhi* (Qianlong ed.), *juan* 170, p. 114.
[91] See Xü Youzhen, *Wugongji* (*siku* ed.), *juan* 5, p. 7.
[92] See Gao Gu, *Yüzhai shiji* (1491 ed.), *juan* 1, p. 5.

Yongle era. He never received any official titles.[93]

Fan Xüan

Fan was known for both his calligraphy and flower-and-bird painting. He entered the court during the Yongle era and served for over thirty years. He won the approval of many scholar officials in court, yet, for some unknown reason, Fan was barred from the promotion granted to all his colleagues in 1414 (see discussion in Chapter One).

Zheng Shimin, Zheng Kegang, Zheng Kang, and Zheng Wenying

Zheng Shimin came from a family of professional painters in Jiangle, Fujian. His father, Zheng Kegang, was a horse and figure painter. In the Xüande era, Kegang was summoned to the court and won great favor with the emperor. However, probably because of his old age, Kegang was honored with the gift of imperial paintings and soon returned home. Instead, his son, Zheng Shimin, also specializing in horse and figure, served for a long time in court. It was recorded that Zheng missed his mother so much he painted a Xüanhuatu depicting the day lily, which is a Chinese symbol for motherly love. Chen received the Jinyiwei title of Zhenfu and later Qianhu. His son, Kang, and his nephew, Wenying, both inherited the family profession. Zheng Kang served as a Jinyi zhenfu during the Zhengtong era. Zheng Wenying's career is not clear, yet a single extant work by him in the Hashimoto collection, dated 1434, demonstrates that he was already an accomplished painter in the late Xüande era.[94]

Shi Rui

Little information is available concerning Shi's biography. According to

---

93 See Lin Huan, *Jiongzhai xiansheng wenji, juan* 1, pp. 3-4 and *juan* 7, pp. 3-4.
94 Hou-mei Sung, "The Symbolic Language of Chinese Horse Painting," *National Palace Museum Bulletin*, v. 36, no. 2 (July 2002), pp. 29-73.

Minghualu, he was a landscape painter serving in the <u>Renzhidian</u> during the Xüande era.[95] Confirming this is the seal indicating his official rank of <u>Jinyi zhenfu</u> on Shi's <u>Tanhuatu</u> in the Hashimoto collection.[96]

He Hao

He Hao, a painter from Guangdong, was known for his paintings of pine trees. He served in the <u>Renzhidian</u> during the Xüande era and received the title of <u>Jinyiwei zhenfu</u>.[97]

Zhou Wenjing and Zhou Ding

Biographical information on Zhou Wenjing is scarce and full of confusion. He appears to have entered the Ming court in the Xuande era (1426-1434) as a <u>Yinyang xünshu</u> (Principal of a District Geomacy). It was recorded that he won first place when Emperor Xüanzong tested new painters with the theme of <u>Gumu hanya</u> (Jackdaws in Old Trees). Yet this did not help Zhou to advance his career as a painter, because Zhou was not officially admitted to the Ming Painting Academy until 1460, when he received his initial salary of five <u>dou</u> of rice. Zhou's continued service as a court painter is suggested by his <u>Gumu hanya</u> in the Shanghai Museum, which contains the seal, Rijin qingguang (Daily Approaching the Radiance), and his <u>Maoshu ailian</u>, dated 1463, which, according to Zhou's own inscription, was painted in the Official Residence of <u>Jintai</u>. The only official title of Zhou, <u>Honglushi xüban</u> (Usher of the Court of State Ceremonial, 9b), was not that of a painter. Yet Zhou's son, Ding, who inherited his position, later received the title of <u>Jinyi zhenfu</u> (5b).[98]

---

[95]   See Xü Xin, *Minghualu, juan* 1, p. 15.

[96]   See Richard Barnhart, *Painters of the Great Ming*, fig. 36.

[97]   He Hao was recorded in both *Guangdong tongzhi* and *Xiyuan cungao, juan* 31, p. 10. For Huang Sheng, see *Xüanzong shilu, juan* 52, p. 6.

[98]   Ibid., *Yingzong shilu, juan* 315, p. 6, and *Minhou xianzhi, juan* 89, p. 2.

Chen Jüe

This undocumented Ming artist was apparently a senior master under the reigns of Yingzong and Jingdi. At the time of his death in 1466, the second year of the Chenghua era, his title was <u>Jinyiwei qianhu</u>. Yet his request for his son to inherit a lower title of <u>Baihu</u> was denied.[99]

Xü Gui

Xü's name is not mentioned in any Ming painting records. Yet new information on Xu's dates and a recently discovered painting confirmed that he was a leading painter in the Chenghua court.[100] As is typical of Ming court painters, Xü first served as a <u>Wensiyuan fushi</u> (Vice Commissioner of the Crafts Institute) in the <u>Renzhidian</u>.[101] In 1482 (the eighteenth year of Chenghua) Xü was promoted from a <u>Jinyiwei suozhenfu</u> (Battalion Judge, 6b) to <u>Fuqianhu</u> (Vice Battalion Commander, 5b). After only two years, in 1484, Xü was again promoted to the rank of <u>Zhengqianhu</u> (Battalion Commander, 5a).[102] The exceptionally rapid promotions of Xü indicate that he must have been a favorite painter of Emperor Xianzong. The dated promotions of Xü also help us to estimate his dates to between 1430s and 1490s.

Lin Liang and Lin Jiao

Like those of most early Ming artists, Lin Liang's biography is brief, with dates varying from source to source. For instance, the starting date for Lin's career in court recorded by *Guangdong xinyu* for the Xuande era (1426-1435) is more than sixty years apart from the Hongzhi era (1488-1505), the date proposed in *Minghualu*. Among the biographical

---

[99]   Ibid., *Xianzong shilu, juan* 31, p. 5.
[100]   The painting signed by Xü Gui depicting a tiger and three cubs is found in the Cincinnati Art Museum (1964.703). The large hanging scroll was mistaken as a Korean painting.
[101]   Xü Gui's title <u>Wensiyuan fushi</u> was inscribed by Xü on the Cincinnati painitng.
[102]   See *Mingshilu, Xianzong shilu, juan* 232, p. 4 and *juan* 257, p. 7.

records concerning Lin, the earliest and most reliable source is the *Guangdong tongzhi*, dated 1550. According to this Ming gazetteer of his hometown, Lin first learned painting with a local master, Yan Zong (1391-1454). The same source also mentioned that as a young man Lin served as a Buzhengshisi zouyi (Assistant in the Provincial Administration Commission) of Guangdong under Commissioner Chen Jin. It was through Chen that Lin's talent in painting was discovered and his reputation among officials known. Although no specific dates were given here, it is possible to estimate Lin's early service under Chen Jin took place between 1455 and 1457, when Chen served in the position of Provincial Administration Commissioner. Lin had apparently already achieved great fame as a painter in Guangdong by this time, as indicated by an inscription by Xiao Zu, dated 1455, on Lin's Jiusitu (Nine Egrets), in which Xiao compared Lin's achievement to that of Bian Wenjin (ca. 1356-1428).

It is likely that Lin entered the court as a painter through the recommendation of Chen Jin shortly after 1457. Lin first served as a Yingshan suocheng (Director of the Construction Office) and worked in the Hall of Renzhidian. According to a poem by Han Yong (1422-1478), a friend of Lin, in 1472 Lin had already reached the honorary ranks of Jinyiwei and served in the court for nine years. In another poem written when Lin was serving as a Jinyi zhenfu, Han pointed out that Lin had been enjoying imperial patronage since the previous reign. It is thus clear that Lin must have started his career in the Tianshun era (1457-1463). This is consistent with the fact that Lin first served as Yingahan suocheng for a period of time before his promotion to the Jinyiwei rank. Han Yong's poem also informs us that in the Chenghua era (1465-1487) while serving as a Jinyiwei zhenfu, Lin was granted a trip home to Guangdong. It is not clear whether Lin was ever promoted to the Jinyiwei zhihui rank. Judging from the above information, it is reasonable to place Lin's dates between 1430s and 1490s.

Lin Jiao, son of Lin Liang, was recruited to the Hongzhi court in 1494, when he won the first place in the imperial contest for painters. Jiao was rewarded the rank of Jinyi zhenfu, which he served until 1504.[103]

Lü Ji (ca. 1420s - 1504)

Lü Ji was a leading flower-and-bird master of the Hongzhi court. His dates have not been found in any Ming records or biographies. Lu's dates, based on new evidences indicating that Lü was promoted from a Baihu (6a) to Fuqianhu (5b) in the tenth month of 1499 and that he died before the third month of 1504, when his son, Tai, was admitted to the Yuyongjian.[104] The new information also led me to question if Lü had ever reached the high rank of Jinyi zhihuishi as recorded in *Minghualu*. How could Lü have climbed from a Fuqianhu (5b) to a Jinyi zhihuishi (3a) within the short period of five years? This is most unlikely considering that, after 1499, waves of strong protests from the Ministries of Personnel, War, Revenue and Rites, as well as censorial officials of the Six Office of Scrutiny and Thirteen Circuits, had not only prevented the emperor from promoting the court painters, but also forced him to demote or eliminate them.[105]

Wu Wei

Wu entered the court in the Hongzhi era, and served as a Jinyi zhenfu in the Renzhidian. But despite his success, Wu returned home after serving only a few years. He was summoned again by Emperor Xiaozong and was offered the title of Jinyi baihu in 1499. The emperor also favored Wu with the seal of huazhuangyuan (the Number One Painter) and later gave him a residence in

---

[103] For discussion of Lin's biography, see Hou-mei Sung, "Lin Liang and His Eagle Painting," *Archives of Asian Art*, XLIV (1991).(quoted as "Lin Liang") and Baozhen Chen, "A Study of Lin Liang and His Paintings," *National Palace Museum Bulletin*, v. XXVII, no. 4.

[104] See Hou-mei Sung, "Lü Chi and His Pheasant Painting," *Gugong xüeshu jikan* (*National Palace Museum Research Quarterly*), *juan.* 10, no. 4 (1993).

[105] See *Ming Shilu, Xiaozong shlu, juan* 155. p. 21; *juan* 157, p. 4 and p. 10; *juan* 159, p. 6 and p. 9; *juan* 160, p. 6; *juan* 162, p. 9; n 164, p. 10; *juan* 165, p. 7; *juan* 175, pp. 6-7; *juan* 178, p. 4; *juan* 180, p. 6; *juan* 188, pp. 5-6; *juan* 197, p. 10; *juan* 198, p. 3; *juan* 211, p. 11; and *juan* 212, p. 5 and 10.

the capital. However, Wu must have sensed the increasing opposition against the imperial patronage of court painters in the late Hongzhi court, because he retired after only three years, claiming it was due to his illness. In the Zhengde era, Wu was once more summoned, but he died before reaching the capital.[106]

Yuan Lin

After an initial period of service as an artisan in the Yuyongjian, Yuan became a Wensiyuan fushi (9b) in the tenth month of 1470. He must have received a promotion to Baihu (6a) between 1470 and 1477, because in the ninth month of 1477, he was promoted from Baihu to Fuqianhu (5b). Three years later, in the tenth month of 1480, he was again promoted to Zhihui qianshi (4a). In less than two years, he had climbed to the high rank of Zhihui tongzhi (3b). In 1485, while serving as a Duzhihui tongzhi, Yuan suffered a temporary salary cut but was soon compensated in 1486 by gaining four clerks. He must have suffered another demotion during the reform of 1487, when all promotions gained through the chuanfeng procedure were retracted.[107]

Lü Wenying

Little is known of Lü Wenying other than that he served in the Hongzhi court and was known as "xiaolü" (Junior Lü) in order to be differentiated from Lü Ji, the "senior Lu." Lü Wenying successfully climbed to the high rank of Zhihui qianshi by the end of the Hongzhi era. Yet in 1505, shortly after his enthronement, Emperor Wuzong succumbed to the continuous protests against the large number of "extra personnel" in court (painters, artisans, imperial relatives, old nannies) and eliminated tow hundred and twenty-four painters and demoted the rest. Lü Wenying suffered a sharp

---

[106]   *Ming Shilu, Xiaozong shilu, juan* 155, p. 9.
[107]   See *Xianzong shilu, juan.* 84, p. 9; *juan* 170, p. 6; *juan* 208, p. 5; *juan* 229, p. 6; and *juan* 265, p. 2.

reduction of two ranks and dropped to the rank of Baihu. However, in 1507, upon his request, the emperor restored his previous rank (Jinyi jianshi). According to Li Rihua, Lü's final rank was Zhihui tongzhi.[108]

Wang E

Wang served as a court painter from the Hongzhi to the Zhengde era. According to *Minghualu*, Wang was promoted to the rank of Jinyi qianhu (5a) in the early Zhengde era (1506-1521). However, this information is challenged by *Mingshilu*, which reveals that in 1510, Wang was promoted from an unranked Zongqi to Suozhenfu (6b). Therefore, Wang must have received his Qianhu near the end of Zhengde era. Additional information comes from a painting in Japan, dated 1541, which suggested that Wang had later reached the higher rank of Jinyi Zhihui.[109]

Zhu Duan

Zhu Duan, a native of Haiyan, Zhejiang, entered the court in 1501 during the late Hongzhi era. In the Zhengde era (1506-1521), he was honored with the high salary of a Jinyi zhihui (Commander of the Embroidered Uniform Guard) and a robe reserved for officials of the highest rank (Jinyi zhihui) in the Zhengde era.[110]

Ji Zhen

According to inscriptions on two of his surviving paintings, Ji once served as a court painter in Wenhuadian as Jinyi qianhu and Jinyi duzhihui.[111]

---

[108]   See *Mingshilu, Wuzong shilu, juan* 30, p. 4.
[109]   For Wang E's biography see, *Wuzong shilu, juan* 70, p. 8 and Richard Barnhart, *Painters of the Great Ming*, p. 260.
[110]   See *Jiaxing fuzhi*, quoted by Mu Yiqin in *Mingdai yuanti zhepai shiliao*, p. 63.
[111]   The two extant paintings by Ji Zhen are Zhuimatu (Falling from the Horse) in Yunnan Provincial Museum and Chunyuan xigou (Dogs Playing in Spring Garden) in a private collection in Japan.

Glossary

Baihu　百戶

Bainiao chaofeng　百鳥朝鳳

Bian Wenjin　邊文進

Bingbu　兵部

Bingke　兵科

Bingke jishizhong　兵科給事中

Buyutu　捕魚圖

Buzhengshisi zouyi　布政使司奏役

Chai Sheng　柴昇

Chen Jin　陳金

Chen Jue　陳玨

Chen Yu　陳遇

Chen Yuan　陳遠

Chen Zongyuan　陳宗淵

Chenghua　成化

Chuanfeng　傳奉

Congma xingchun　驄馬行春

Daizhao　待詔

Dashi　大使

Diziyuan　弟子員

Donggong　東宮

Dongzhi yiyang　多至一陽

Dou　斗

Duzhihui qianshi　都指揮僉事

Duzhihui tongzhi 都指揮同知
Duzhihuishi 都指揮使
Exi 鵝溪
Fan Xian 范暹
Fang Changling 方昌齡
Fang Liangbi 方良弼
Fujian 福建
Fujun qianwei 府軍前衛
Fuqianhu 副千戶
Fushi 副使
Fuyü 富峪
Gemenshi 閣門使
Geng Yü 耿裕
Gongbu 工部
Gongke 工科
Gongke jishizhong   工科給事中
Guandai 冠帶
Guandai xiaoqi 冠帶小旗
Guandai zongqi 冠帶總旗
Guangeti 館閣體
Guangdong tongzhi 廣東通志
Guangdong xinyu 廣東新語
Guanjiang 官匠
Gumu hanya 古木寒鴉
Guo Chun 郭純
Guo Wentong 郭文通
Guozi xuezheng 國子學正
Haiyan 海鹽
Han Xiushi 韓秀實
Hanlin 翰林

Hanlin bianxiu 翰林編修

He Hao 何浩

Honglusi xuban 鴻臚寺序班

Hongwu 洪武

Hongxi 洪熙

Hongzhi 弘治

Huagong 畫工

Huaien 懷恩

Huang Huai 黃淮

Huang Sheng 黃勝

Huang Si 黃賜

Huang Taisun 皇太孫

Huayuan 畫院

Huazhuangyuan 畫狀元

Hubu 戶部

Jiajing 嘉靖

Jiang Zicheng 蔣子成

Jiashen shitongniantu 甲申十同年圖

Jin Ying 金英

Jin Zhong 金忠

Jingdi 景帝

Jingtai 景泰

Jinmen huashi 金門畫史

Jinmen shiyu 金門侍御

Jinshi 進士

Jintai 金台

Jinwuwei 金吾衛

Jinwuyouwei 金吾右衛

Jinyi qianhu zhizhang 錦衣千戶之章

Jinyi zhenfu 錦衣鎮撫

Jinyi zhihui 錦衣指揮
Jinyiwei 錦衣衛
Jinzhong sanjue 禁中三絕
Jishizhong 給事中
Jiusitu 九鷺圖
Jün 軍
Jungong 軍功
Junjiang 軍匠
Li Rihua 李日華
Li Rong 李榮
Libu 吏部
Lin Huan 林環
Lin Jiao 林郊
Lin Liang 林良
Liu Jie 劉節
Liu Jin 劉晉
Liu Jun 劉俊
Liu Xin 劉信
Longshan 隆善
Lü Ji 呂紀
Lü Wenying 呂文英
Lu Yi 陸釴
Maoshu ailian 茂叔愛蓮
Min Gui 閔珪
Ming 明
Minghualu 明畫錄
Mingsheng 明昇
Mingshilu 明實錄
Minjiang 民匠
Minzhe 閩浙

Ni Duan 倪端

Ning Zhen 寧禎

Ning Zhong 寧忠

Pinpangtu 聘龐圖

Qianhu 千戶

Qianhusuo 千戶所

Qidong 啓東

Qinjun zhihui shisi 親軍指揮使司

Qintianjian 欽天監

Qiu Jun 邱濬

Rehe 熱河

Renzhidian 仁智殿

Renzong 仁宗

Rijin qingguang 日近清光

Ruan Lang 阮浪

Shang Xi 商喜

Shangguan boda 上官伯達

Shaoshi 少師

Shaoxing 紹興

Shen Xiyuan 沈希遠

Shenzong 神宗

Sheren 舍人

Shezhitu 射雉圖

Shi Rui 石銳

Shibaihu 試百戶

Shizhihuifeng 食指揮俸

Shizong 世宗

Shoujinyiwei fuqianhufeng 授錦衣衛副千戶俸

Shuangxitu 雙喜圖

Shuyiju 書藝局

Shuyuan 書院
Silijian 司禮監
Suichao jiazhao 歲朝佳兆
Suihantu 歲寒圖
Sun Ke 孫恪
Sun Long 孫隆
Sun Wenzong 孫文宗
Sun Xingzu 孫興祖
Suocheng 所丞
Suofu 所副
Suozhenfu 所鎮撫
Tan Chang 覃昌
Tianshun 天順
Tumu 土木
Wang E 王諤
Wang Fu 王紱
Wang Shuan 王叔安
Wang Xianzhi 王獻之
Wang Xizhi 王羲之
Wang Zhao 王詔
Wang Zhen 王鎮
Wanli 萬曆
Wei Chun 蔚春
Wei Tai 韋泰
Weizhenfu 衛鎮撫
Wenhuadian 文華殿
Wensiyuan 文思院
Wenyuange 文淵閣
Wu 武
Wu Wei 吳偉

Wugong youwei 武功右衛

Wugong zhongwei 武功中衛

Wugong Zuowei 武功左衛

Wujun dudufu 五軍都督府

Wulou 武樓

Wuluntu 五倫圖

Wuyingdian 武英殿

Wuzong 武宗

Xia 夏

Xia Chang 夏昶

Xianzong 憲宗

Xiao Jing 蕭敬

Xiao Zi 蕭鎡

Xiaoqi 小旗

Xiaozong 孝宗

Xie Huan 謝環

Xie Jin 解縉

Xihuameng 西華門

Xingwu 興武

Xingyuan 杏園

Xu Gui 徐貴

Xu Lin 徐麟

Xu Ying 徐英

Xuande 宣德

Xüanhuatu 萱花圖

Xüanzong 宣宗

Xüanzong shelietu 宣宗射獵圖

Xüanzong shilu 宣宗實錄

Yan Song 嚴嵩

Yan Zong 顏宗

Yanshanhou 燕山侯
Yang Rong 楊榮
Yang Shiqi 楊士奇
Yao Guangxiao 姚廣孝
Yin Hong 殷宏
Yin Shan 殷善
Yin Shun 殷順
Yin Xie 殷偕
Yingji tiane 鷹擊天鵝
Yingshan 營繕
Yingshansuo 營繕所
Yingshansuo cheng 營繕所丞
Yingxiong duojin 鷹熊奪錦 (英雄奪錦)
Yingzong 英宗
Yinyang xunshu 陰陽訓術
Yituan heqi 一團和氣
Yongjia 永嘉
Yongle 永樂
Youjishizhong 右給事中
Yü Shan 俞山
Yuan 元
Yuan Lin 袁林
Yuan Zhongche 袁忠徹
Yülin qianwei 羽林前衛
Yüshuyuan 御書院
Yüyongjian 御用監
Yüyongsi 御用司
Zhang Bao 張寶
Zhang Ji 張玘
Zhang Jin 張錦

Zhang Jing 張靖

Zhang Ning 張寧

Zhao Fu 趙福

Zhao Hu 趙虎

Zhao Lian 趙廉

Zhao Linsu 趙麟素

Zhao Yuan 趙原

Zhenfu 鎮撫

Zheng Kang 鄭康

Zheng Kegang 鄭克鋼

Zheng Shimin 鄭時敏

Zheng Wenying 鄭文英

Zhengde 正德

Zhengqianhu 正千戶

Zhengtong 正統

Zhihui 指揮

Zhihui qianshi 指揮僉事

Zhihuishi 指揮使

Zhihui tongzhi 指揮同知

Zhonghou 中後

Zhongqian 中前

Zhongshu 中書

Zhongshusheng 中書省

Zhongshu sheren 中書舍人

Zhongyou 中右

Zhongzhong 中中

Zhongzuo 中左

Zhou 周

Zhou Ding 周鼎

Zhou Qüan 周全

Zhou Wenjing　周文靖

Zhou Xuan　周旋

Zouyütu　騶虞圖

Zhu Duan　朱端

Zhu Fei　朱芾

Zhou Houzhao　朱厚照

Zhu Jianshen　朱見深

Zhu Kongyang　朱孔陽

Zhu Qiyü　朱祁鈺

Zhu Yan　朱鈗

Zhu Yunwen　朱允炆

Zhu Zhanji　朱瞻基

Zongqi　總旗

Selected Bibliography

Abbreviations

CL – Rare Book collection of National Central Library, Taipei, Taiwan:

HPCS – Huapin congshu. Shanghai: Shanghai Renmin Publishing Company, 1982.

HSCS – Huashi congshu. Taipei: Wenshizhe Publishing Company, 1974

SKQS – Siku quanshu (Complete Library in Four Branches of Literature). 1773-1785.

YSCB -- Yishu congbian, Taipei, preface 1962

Books in Chinese and Japanese

Cao Boqi. *Cao wenzhengong shiji*. SKQS ed.

Cao Xüeqüan. *Shicang lidai shixüan*. SKQS ed.

Ch'en Fang-mei. *Daijin yanjiu*. Taipei: National Palace Museum, 1981.

Chen Gaohua. *Songliaojin huajia shiliao*. Beijing: Wenwu Publishing Company, 1984.

Chen Hongmo, *Gaowu shigao*. 1534 ed. CL.

Chen Ji. *Yibaizhai gao*. SKQS ed.

Chen Jingzong. *Tanran jushiji*. 1522-1566 ed. CL.

Chen Yan. *Yuanshi jishi*. Taipei, 1971.

Chen Zhi. *Shenduso yigao*. SKQS ed.

Cheng Jüfu. *Chengxüelouji*. SKQS ed.

Cheng Minzheng. *Huangdun wenji*. SKQS ed.

Cheng Wende. *Chengwengong wenji*. 1573-1620 ed. CL.

Choshunkaku Kansho. Tokyo, 1944.

Daxin (monk). *Pushiji*. SKQS ed.

Dai Xu. *Wanchuanji*. SKQS ed.

Deng Chun. *Huaji*. (in HSCS series), Taipei, 1974.

Ding Fu. *Kuaitingji*. SKQS ed.

Dong You. *Guangchuan huaba* (in HPCS series). Shanghai: People's Art
    Publishing Company 1982.

Fang Yue. *Qiuyaiji*. SKQS ed.

Fei Hong. *Fei Wenxian gong zhaigao*. Ming ed. CL.

Feng Fang. *Feng Gaogong yiji*. 1573-1620 ed. CL.

Gao Bing. *Xiaotaiji*. Ming ed. CL.

Gao Gu. *Yüzhai shiji*. 1491 ed. CL.

Gong Kui. *Yunlinji*. SKQS ed.

Gu Fu. *Pingsheng zhuangguan*. Shanghai: 1962.

Gu Qing. *Dongjiang jiacangji*. 1522-1566 ed. CL.

Guan Fuqu. *Guhua liuzhen*. Shanghai, 1916

Gugong shuhua tulu (Painting Catalogue of the National PalaceMuseum,
    Taipei): National Palace Museum, Taipei, Taiwan 1990.

Guo Zizhang. *Mingmaji*. Ming ed. of National Central Library

Guo Pu. *Shanhaijing jianshu*. Taipei: Chung Hwa Book Company, 1971.

Guo Ruoxu. *Tuhua jianwanzhi*. (in HSCS series). Taipei, 1974.

Guo Xiangzheng. *Qingshanji*. SKQS ed.

Guo Yu. *Jingsiji*. SKQS ed.

Guochao xianzhenglu (A Collection of Ming Biographies),Photolithographic
    ed., Taipei, 1965.

Han Yong. *Xiangyi wenji*. SKQS ed.

Hao Jing. *Lingchuanji*. SKQS ed.

He Jingming. *Dafuji*. SKQS ed.

He Xiu. *Chunqiu gongyang jiegu*. Shanghai, 1929.

Hou Kezhong. *Kenzhaiji*. SKQS ed.

Hou Yiyuan. *Ergu shanrenji, lingnanji*. Ming ed. CL.

Hu Song. *Zhuangsugong yigao*. SKQS ed.

Hu Yan. *Yian wenxuan*. 1522-1566 ed. CL.

Hu Zhiyü. *Zishan taquanji*. SKQS ed.

Huai-an County Museum and the Group for the Authentication of Ancient Works of Chinese Painting and Calligraphy. *Huai-an Mingmu chutu shuhua*. Beijing: Wenwu Publishing Co., 1988.

Huang Huai. *Jieanji* (in *Jingxianglou congshu*). Taipei: Wenshizhe Publishing Company, 1974.

Huang Runyu. *Nanshan huangxiansheng jiacangji*. Ming ed. CL.

Huang Xiufu. *Yizhou minghualu*. Chengdu, 1982

Jiang Shaoshu. *Wusheng Shishi*. (in HSCS series). Taipei, 1974.

Jiang Yida. *Wupo wenji*. 1571 ed. CL.

Jie Xisi. *Wenanji*. SKQS ed.

Ke Qian. *Zhuyanji*. SKQS ed.

Kohara, Hironobu. "Wild Geese and Reeds." *Kobijutsu*, no. 27 (September, 1969), pp. 93-97.

Li Angying. *Wenxiji*. SKQS ed.

Li Dongyang. *Lidongyang ji*. Changsha: Yuelu Book Company, 1984.

Li Fang. *Taiping guangji*. Taipei, 1969.

Li Jian. *Deyüzhai huapin*. (in HPCS series). Shanghai: People's Art Publishing Company, 1982.

Li Jünmin. *Zhuangjingji*. SKQS ed.

Li Peng. *Risheyüanji*. SKQS ed.

Li Qixian. *Yizhaiji*. *Yueyatang congshu* ed.

Li Shi. *Fangzhouji*. SKQS ed.

Li Tianma. "Linliang niandai kao." *Yilin congshu* III (1962), pp. 35-38.

Li Weizhen. *Dami shanfangji*. Ming ed. CL.

Liang Chu. *Yuzhou yigao*. 1522-1566 ed. CL.

Lin Bi. *Lindengzhou ji*. SKQS ed.

Lin Huan. *Jiongzhai xiansheng wenji*. Ming ed. CL.

Lin Zhi. *Xuke buzhaigong wenji*. 1573-1620 ed. CL.

Linliang Luji huaji (Collection of Paintings of Lin Liang and Lu Ji). Tianjin: People's Fine Arts House, 1997.

Ling Zhen. *Lianxiji*, 1551 ed. CL.

Liu Ban. *Pengchengji*. SKQS ed.

Liu Caishao. *Shanxi Jüshiji*. SKQS ed.

Liu Daochun. *Shengchao minghua ping*. (in HPCS series). Shanghai: People's Art Publishing Company, 1982.

Liu Dingzhi. *Daizhai cungao*. Ming ed. CL.

Liu Ji. Liu *Wenchenggong wenji*. SKQS ed.

Liu Minzhong. *Zhonganji*. SKQS ed.

Liu Qiu. *Liangxi wenji*. SKQS ed.

Liu Xüeji. *Fang Shixian jushi xiaogao*. SKQS ed.

Liu Yi. *Guzhi xiansheng wenji*. 1524 ed. CL.

Lo Qinshun. *Zhengan cungao*. SKQS ed.

Lu Dian. *Piya*. SKQS ed.

Lü Nangong. *Guanyuanji*. SKQS ed.

Lu Rong. *Guitiangao*. Ming ed. CL.

Lu Yi. *Chunyü tanggao*. Ming ed. CL.

Lü Yuan. *Lü Wenyi gong qüanji*. CL.

Luo Lun. *Yifeng xiansheng wenji*. SKQS ed.

Ming Huiyao (Handbook on Ming Government). Typeset ed., Beijing: Zhonghua Book Company, 1956.

Ming Renzong shilu (Veritable Record of the Ming Hongxi period). Taipei, 1963.

Ming Taizong shilu (Veritable Record of the Ming: Yongle period). Taipei, 1963.

Ming Taizu shilu (Veritable Record of the Ming: Hongwu period). Taipei,

1963.

Ming Wuzong shilu (Veritable Record of the Ming Zhengde period). Taipei, 1963.

Ming Xuanzong shilu (Veritable Record of the Ming: Xuande period). Taipei, 1963.

Ming Yingzong shilu (Veritable Record of the Ming Zhengtong period). Taipei, 1963.

Mingdai gongting yü zhepai huihua xüanji. Beijing: National Palace Museum, Wenwu Publishing Company, 1983.

Mingqing renwu xiaoxiang huaxuan. Shanghai: People's Art Publishing Company, 1982.

Minzhong shuhualu. Jiajing era (1796-1820) ed.

Mu Yiqin. *Mingdai yuanti zhepai shiliao.* Shanghai, 1985.

Mingren zhuanji ziliao suoyin. Taipei: National Central Library, 1965.

Ni Qian. *Niwenxiji.* SKQS ed.

Ouyang Xuan. *Guizhaiji.* SKQS ed.

Pei Xiaoyuan. *Zhenguan gongsi huashi.* (in HPCS series). Shanghai: People's Art Publishing Company, 1982.

Pu Daoyuan. *Xiznju conggao.* SKQS ed.

Qiu Jün. *Qiongtaigao.* SKQS ed.

Sang Yue. *Sixuanji.* 1573-11620 ed. CL.

Seikai Bijutsu Zenshu. Tokyo: Heibon-sha, 1929

Shi Jun. *Lianquan shiji.* Ming ed. CL.

Shijing. sibu congkan ed. Shanghai, 1929.

Shoheikiga Zenshu. Tokyo: Bijutsu Shupensha, 1966-87.

Sogen Chugoku Kaigaten (Exhibition of Sung-Yuan Chinese Paintings). Homma Art Museum. Yamagata, 1979.

Sogen no Kaiga (Chinese Painting of the Song and Yuan Dynasties). Tokyo National Museum. Benrido, 1962.

Songren zhuangji ziliao suoyin (Dictionary of Song Biographies). Taipei:

Dingwen Book Co., 1986.

Su Song. *Suweigong wenji.* SKQS ed.

Sun Chengen. *Wenjianji.* SKQS ed.

Sun Chengze. *Gengzi xiaoxiaji.* SKQS ed.

Sun Shaoyuan. *Shenghuaji.* SKQS ed.

Sun Yi. *Dongting yürenji.* Ming ed. CL.

Suzuki Kei. *Mindai kaigashi no kenkyu: Seppa* (A Study of Ming Painting: the Zhe School), Toyo bunka Kenkyujo Kiyo (special issue 1968).

_____. "Concerning the Organization of the Ming Painting Academy." *Bijutsushi*, v. 15, no. 4 (March 1955), 95-106.

_____. *Comprehensive Illustrated Catalogue of Chinese Painting.* Tokyo: 1982-3, 5 vols.

Tang Hou. Huajian (in HPCS series). Shanghai: People's Art   Publishing Company, 1982.

Tang Guifang. *Baiyunji.* SKQS ed.

Tangsong yuanming minghua daguan, Tokyo, 1929.

Tang Wenfeng. *Wugangji*   SKQS ed.

Tao Liang. *Hongdou shuguan shuhuaji* (prefaced 1836). Taipei: Hanhua Publishing Company, 1972.

Toda Teisuke. "Ryu Setsu hitsu Sogyo zu ni tsuite." (Some Notes on Liu Jie's "Fish and Water Plants"). *Bijutsu Kenkyu*, 243 (November, 1965), 18-25.

Tong Shu. *Jüanji.* SKQS ed.

Tong Xuan. *Qingfeng tinggao.* SKQS ed.

Wang Ao. *Zhenzeji.* SKQS ed.

Wang Gong. *Baiyun qiaochangji.* SKQS ed.

Wang Keyu. *Shanhuwang hualu.* Shanghai, 1936.

Wang Li. *Linyüan wenji.* SKQS ed.

Wang Wensheng. *Wang Baiquan xianshenggao.* Ming ed. CL.

Wang Xü. *Lanxuanji.* SKQS ed.

Wang Ying. *Wang Wenangong shiji* 1465 ed. CL.

Wang Youdun. *Songquanji*. SKQS ed.

Wang Yuxian. *Huishi beikao*. SKQS ed.

Wang Zhi. *Wang Wenduangong wenji*. SKQS ed.

Wang Zudi. *Shizhutangji*. SKQS ed..

Wen Jia. *Qianshantang shuhuaji* (in *Yishu congbian* series). Taipei: Shijie Book Company, 1977.

Wu Cheng. *Wuwenzheng ji* SKQS ed.

Wudai Wangchuzhi mu (Wang Chuzhi's Tomb of the Five Dynasties Period), Cultural Relics Publishing House, Beijing, 1998.

Wu Kuan. *Jiacangji*. SKQS ed.

Wu Qiuyan. *Zhusu shanfang shiji*. SKQS ed.

Wu Qizhen. *Shuhuaji*. Shanghai, 1963.

Wu Sheng. *Daguanlu*. Reprint, Taipei, 1960.

Wu Shidao. *Libuji*. SKQS ed.

Wu Zhihe. "Tumu zhibian hou mingchao yü wala zhijiaoshe," *Mingshi yanjiu zhuankan*, v. 3, pp. 75.

Xia Liangsheng. *Dongzhou chugao*. SKQS ed.

Xia Wenyan. *Tuhui baojian xubian*. (in HSCS series). Taipei, 1974.

Xiao Yü. *Yexiacao*. 1573-1620 ed. CL.

Xu Fei. *Meiwuji*. SKQS ed.

Xu Lun. *Shezhaiji*. SKQS ed.

Xu Xin. *Minghualu*. (in HSCS series). Taipei, 1974.

Xu Youren. *Zhizhengji*. SKQS ed.

Xü Youzhen. *Wugongji*. SKQS ed.

Xuanhe huapu. (in *Huashi congshu* series). Taipei: Xuesheng Book Company, 1971.

Yang Chenbin. "Yuandai Ren Renfa ermatu juan." *Wenwu*, 1965, No. 8, pp. 34-36.

Yang Rong. *Wenminji*. SKQS ed.

Yang Shiqi. *Dongli wenji* and *xuji*. SKQS ed.

Yang Shouchen. *Yang wenyigong wenji*. 1573-1620 ed. CL.

Yang Yiqing. *Shizong shikao*. SKQS ed.

Yang Yingchun, *Buzhuoji*, 1441 ed. CL.

Yao Zhiyin. *Yuanmingshi leichao*. SKQS ed.

Ye Sheng. *Shuidong riji*. (in *Yuanmingshi biji congkan*), Beijing: Zhonghua Book Company, 1980, reprint.

Yiyuan duoying (An Illustrated Journal of Chinese Painting and Calligraphy). Shanghai: People's Art Publishing Company, since 1978.

Yü Ji. *Daoyuan yigao*. SKQS ed.

Yü Kan. *Yudanyuan shiji*. SKQS ed.

Yu Menglin. *Yu xueshiji*. 1573-1620 ed. CL.

Yu Shenxing. *Gushan bichen*. 1573-1620 ed. CL.

Yuan Xie. *Xiezhaiji*. SKQS ed.

Yuanshi jishi. Shanghai: Shanghai Guji Publishing Company, 1971.

Yuanren zhuanji ziliao suoyin (Dictionary of Yuan Biographies). Taipei: Xinwenfeng Publishing Company, 1979.

Yuesheng suocang shuhua pielu. YSCB ed..

Zhang Bochun. *Yangmeng wenji*. SKQS ed.

Zhang Jiucheng. *Hengpuji*. SKQS ed.

Zhang Jü., *Jianghu houji*. SKQS ed.

Zhang Kui. *Yunan xiansheng shiji*. 1564 ed. CL.

Zhang Lei, *Keshanji*. SKQS ed.

Zhang Ning. *Fangzhouji*. SKQS ed.

Zhang Qi. *Xiyuanji*. Ming ed. CL.

Zhang Yanyuan. *Lidai minghuaji* (in *Huashi congshu* series). Taipei: Xuesheng Book Company, 1971.

Zhang Yong. *Guaiyaiji*. SKQS ed.

Zhang Zhe. *Tuixuanji*. Ming ed. CL.

Zhao Han. *Jianzhai Shicao*. Ming ed. CL.

Zhao Yongxian. *Songshizhaiji*. 1573-1620 ed. CL.

Zheng Shanfu. *Shaogu quanji*. SKQS ed.

Zheng Wenkang. *Pingqiaogao*. SKQS ed.

Zheng Xie. *Yunxiji*. SKQS ed.

Zheng Xuan. *Zhou Li*. Shanghai, 1929.

Zhongguo huaxiangshi quanji (Collection of Chinese Carved Stone Relief). Henan Fine Art Publihsing Company, 2000.

Zhongguo meishu quanji, huihua bian. Shanghai, 1988, 21 volumes.

Zhongguo minghuaji. Shanghai, 1923..

Zhongwen dacidian (The Encyclopedic Dictionary of the Chinese Language). Taipei: Chinese Cultural University, 1990 reprint.

Zhou Beqi. *Jinguangji*. SKQS ed.

Zhou Mi. *Yünyan guoyanlu* (in YSCB series). Taipei, 1977.

Zhou Qi. *Xiyuanji*. Ming ed. CL.

Zhou Tingzhen. *Shichuji*. Ming ed. CL.

Zhou Zizhi. *Taicang timiji*. Ming ed. CL.

Zhu Chengyong. *Xiaominggao*. SKQS ed.

Zhu Jian. *Yuanxuegao*. Ming ed. CL.

Zhu Jingxuan. *Tangchao minghualu* (in HPCS series). Shanghai: People's Art Publishing Company, 1982.

Zhu Rangxu. *Changchun jingchengao*. 1573-1620 ed. CL.

Zhu Yi. *Qianshanji*   SKQS ed.

Zhu Yünming. *Zhushi jilüe*. Taipei, 1971.

Zong Dian. "Yuan Ren Renfa muzhi difaxian, (The discovery of the epitaph of Ren Renfa)." *Wenwu*, 1959, No. 11.

Zongle. *Quanshi waiji*. SKQS ed.

Zou Shouyi. *Zou dongguo xiansheng shiji*. 1573-1620 ed. CL.

Books and Series in Western Languages

Forke, Alfred. *The World-Conception of the Chinese: Their Astronomical, Cosmological and Physio-Philosophical Speculations.* London: Probsthain, 1925.

Akiyama Terukazu. "Deux Peintures de Touen-Houang, sur soie, representant un Pelerin Portrait des sutras et accompagne d'un Tigre." *Bijutsu Kenkyu*, no. 238 (1964); 163-183; and "An Yuan Painting of Eighteen Arhats." Bijutsu Kenkyu, no. 261.

Arnold, Lauren. *Princely Gifts and Papal Treasures: The Franciscan Mission to China and Its Influence on the Art of the West 1250-1350.* San Francisco, 1999.

Barnhart, Richard. *Painters of the Great Ming.* Dallas Museum of Art, 1993.

Cahill, James. *An Index of Early Chinese Painters and Paintings: T'ang and Song.* Berkeley: University of California Press, 1980.

_____. *Hills Beyond a River: Chinese Painting of the Yuan Dynasty 1279-1368.* New York and Tokyo: Weatherhill, 1976.

_____. *Parting at the Shore: Chinese Painting of the Early and Middle Ming Dynasty 1368-1580.* New York and Tokyo: Weatherhill, 1978.

Ch'en, Pao-chen "A Study of Lin Liang and His Paintings," National Palace *Museum Bulletin*, v. XXVII, no. 4.

Chinese Paintings of the Yüan Dynasty on Buddhist and Taoist Figure Subjects. Tokyo National Museum, 1975.

Eight Dynasties of Chinese Painting: the Collections of the Nelson Gallery-Atkins Museum, Kansas Cit, and the Cleveland Museum of Art. Cleveland: Cleveland Museum of Art, 1980.

Farmer, Edward L. *Early Ming Government: The Evolution of Dual Capitals*, Cambridge: Harvard University Press, 1976.

Fontein, Jan and Hickman, Money L. *Zen Painting and Calligraphy.* Museum of Fine Arts, Boston, 1970.

Forke, Alfred. *The World-Conception of the Chinese: Their Astronomical, Cosmological and Physio-Philosophical Speculations. London: Probs thain,* 1925.

Garrett, Valery M. *Chinese Clothing, An Illustrated Guide.* Oxford and New York: Oxford University Press, 1994.

Goodrich, L. Carrington ed. *Dictionary of Ming Biography.* New York and London: Columbia University Press, 1976.

Hartman, Charles. "literary and Visual Interactions in Lo Chi-ch'uan's Crows in Old Trees." *The Metropolitan Museum Journal,* 28 (1993), 129-167.

Hucker, Charles O. *A Dictionary of Official Titles in Imperial China.* Standford: Standford University Press, 1985.

Lee, Sherman and Ho, Wai-kam. *Chinese Art under the Mongols,* the Cleveland Museum of Art, 1968.

Lee, Sherman E. "Early Ming Painting at the Imperial Court." *The Bulletin of the Cleveland Museum of Art* XLIII (October 1975), 243-59.

_____. "Literati and Professionals: Four Ming Painters." *The Bulletin of the Cleveland Museum of Art* LIII (January 1966), 2-25.

_____. "The Tiger and Dragon Screens by Sesson." The Bulletin of the Cleveland Museum of Art, XLVII (April 1960).

Legge, James. *The Four Books.* Shanghai: The Chinese Book Company, 1930.

Li Chu-tsing. "The Freer Sheep and Goat and Chao Meng-fu's Horse Paintings," *Artibus Asiae,* XXX, No. 4 (1968), 279-346.

Loehr, Max. " Chinese paintings with Sung Dated Inscriptions. " *Ars Orientalis* IV, 1961, 247.

Maeda, Robert. "The Water Theme in Chinese Painting." *Artibus Asiae,* v. 33, no.4 (1971), 247-266.

Mino, Yutaka. *Freedom of Clay and Brush through Seven Centuries in Northern China: Cizhou Type Wares, 960-1600 A.D.* Indiana: Indiana University Press, 1981.

Mino, Yutaka and Robinson, James. *Beauty and Tranquillity: The Eli Lilly Collection of Chinese Art*. Indianapolis Museum of Art, 1983.

Murray, Julia K. *Ma Hezhi and the Illustration of the Book of Odes*. Cambridge University Press, 1993.

Rosenfield, John M. and Shimada, Shujiro. *Traditions of Japanese Art: Selections from the Kimiko and John Powers Collection*. Fogg Art Museum and Harvard University, 1970.

Rowland, Benjamin. "Hui-tsung and Huang Ch'uan." *Artibus Asiae*, XVII (1954), 131-133.

Sakanishi, Shio. *The Spirit of the Brush*. London, 1939.

Schirokauer, Conrad. *A Brief History of Chinese Civilization*. Orlando: Harcourt Brace Jovanovich, Inc., 1991.

Shih Shou-ch'ien. "Che School Painting Style and Aristocratic Taste." *Soochow University Journal of Chinese Art History*, v. 15 (July 1985), 307-342.

Siggstedt, Mette. "Zhou Chen: The Life and Paintings of a Ming Professional Artist." *The Museum of Far Eastern Antiquities Bulletin* 54 (1982).

Siren, Osvald. *Chinese Painting*. New York and London, 1956, 7 volumes.

Soper, Alexander. *Guo Roxu's Experience in Painting*, Washington, D.C.:American Council of Learned Societies, 1951.

Sung Hou-mei. "Bian Wenjin and His Flower-and-bird Painting." *Oriental Art*, n.s., n. XXXVIII, no. 3 (Autumn 1992), 154-164.

Primary Chinese and Japanese Sources

_____. "Early Ming Painters in Nanking and the Formation of the Wu School." *Ars Orientalis*, XVII (1988), 73-115.

_____. "From the Min-Che Tradition to the Che School, Part 2: Precursors of the Che School, Hsieh Huan and Tai Chin" *the National Palace Museum Research Quarterly*, v. 7, no. 1 (1989), 6-10.(cited as "Min-Che, Part 2."

_____. "The Formation of the Ming Painting Academy. " *Ming Studies*, no. 29 (spring 1991), 30.

_____. "Lin Liang and His Eagle Painting." *Archives of Asian Art*, XLIV (1991), 95-102.

_____. "Lü Chi and His Pheasant Painting. " *National Palace Museum Research Quarterly*, v. 10, no. 4 (summer 1993), 1-22.

_____. "The Evolution of Chinese Pigeon Painting. " *Oriental Art*, v. XXXIX, no. 3 (autumn 1993), 28-38.

_____. "The Eagle Painting Themes of the Ming Court. " *Archives of Asian Art*, XLVIII (1995), 48-63.

_____. "Chinese Fish Painting of the Sung and Yuan Dynasties and Its Symbolic Meanings. " *National Palace Museum Bulletin*, v. XXX, no. 1 & 2 (May-June, 1995), 1.

_____. "Chinese Fish Painting of the Ming Dynasty and Its Symbolic Meanings. " *National Palace Museum Bulletin*, v. XXX, no. 3 & 4 (July-August, September-October, 1995), p. 1.

_____. " "Wild Geese and Reeds Painting (Lu-yen t'u) of the Ming Court. " *Oriental Art* v.XLII, no. 1 (Spring, 1996), 30-42.

_____. "Crane in Chinese Painting. " *Oriental Art*, v. XLIV, no. 3 (1998), 11-23.

_____. "Chinese Tiger Painting Themes and Their Symbolic Meanings." Part 1 and Part 2, *National Palace Museum Bulletin*, v. XXXIII, no. 4 (September-October 1998), pp. 1-17; and v. XXXIII, no. 5, (November-December 1998), 17-33.

_____. "The Three Yin Masters of the Ming Court: Yin Shan, Yin Hsieh, and Yin Hung." *Artibus Asiae*, v. LVIII, no. 1/2 (1998), 91-113.

_____. "The Symbolic Language of Chinese Horse Painting. " *National Palace Museum Bulletin*, v. 36, no. 2 (July 2002), 29-73.

Vanderstappen, Harry. "Painters at the Early Ming Court and the Problem of a Ming Painting Academy. " *Monumenta Serica*, v. 15 (1956), 259-302 and v. 16 (1957), 315-347.

Waley, Arthur. *The Book of Songs.*   New York, 1960.

Watson, Burton. *The Complete Works of Zhuang Zi.* New York: Columbia University Press, 1964.

Wu Tung. *Tales from the Land of Dragons: 1000 Years of Chinese Painting.* Exhibition Catalogue Boston: Museum of Fine Arts, 1997.

Yoshiaki Shimizu and Carolyn Wheelwright (eds.). *Japanese Ink Paintings.* Princeton: Princeton University Press, 1976.

The Unknown World of the Ming Court
Painters: The Ming Painting Academy 日
近清光 / By Hou-mei Sung 宋后楣著.– 初版. --
臺北市：文史哲, 民 95
面： 公分.（藝術叢刊；18）
參考書目：面
ISBN 957-549-649-3 (平裝)

1.中國美術史 – 明（1368-1644）

909.26

藝 術 叢 刊　18

The Unknown World of the Ming Court
Painters: The Ming Painting Academy
日　近　清　光

著　　　者：Hou-mei Sung　宋　后　楣
出 版 者：文　史　哲　出　版　社
　　　　　http://www.lapen.com.tw
登記證字號：行政院新聞局版臺業字五三三七號
發 行 人：彭　　　　正　　　　雄
發 行 所：文　史　哲　出　版　社
印 刷 者：文　史　哲　出　版　社
臺北市羅斯福路一段七十二巷四號
郵政劃撥帳號：一六一八〇一七五
電話886-2-23511028 ‧ 傳真886-2-23965656

定價新臺幣二四〇元 美金八元

中華民國九十五年（2006）元月初版

ISBN 957-549-649-3　　　91118